DR. GRAMMAR'S
WRITES
FROM
WRONGS

DR. GRAMMAR'S
WRITES
FROM
WRONGS

A Supremely Authoritative Guide
to the Common and Not-So-Common
Rules of the English Language

BY

DR. GRAMMAR
(Richard Francis Tracz)

PRODUCED BY

JEROME AGEL

Vintage Books
A Division of Random House, Inc.
New York

A VINTAGE ORIGINAL

First Edition, September 1991

Copyright © 1991 by Jerome Agel

Library of Congress Cataloging-in-Publication Data
Tracz, Richard Francis.
Dr. Grammar's writes from wrongs / by Dr. Grammar (Richard
Francis Tracz); produced by Jerome Agel.—1st ed.
p. cm.
"A Vintage original"—T.p. verso.
ISBN 0-679-72715-9
1. English language—Grammar—1950– . 2. English
language—Usage.
I. Title.
PE1106.T7 1991
428.2—dc20   90-46544
CIP

Book design by Rebecca Aidlin

Manufactured in the United States of America
10 9 8 7 6 5 4

FOR BOLEY AND FRANCES

ACKNOWLEDGMENTS

First of all, I want to thank the countless callers who provided me with the questions for this book. Without them, I would have no "writes" and wrongs to discuss with you.

Secondly, a note of thanks and deep appreciation to C. Jeriel Howard, a prominent rhetorician and teacher of English. Our lively discussions about grammar and usage have helped me to appreciate the ambiguity—a source of both consolation and frustration—of the English language. His support has been immeasurable.

Finally, no book of mine would be complete without thanking Pretza and Herr Schmitz. Their constant companionship, especially in times of physical or emotional crisis, has been a comfort and a source of strength. Bless them.

—Richard Francis Tracz
("Dr. Grammar")
Chicago, 1991

CONTENTS

INTRODUCTION

XIII

SECTION ONE:

IN WHICH DR. GRAMMAR ANSWERS QUESTIONS ABOUT GRAMMAR

1

PARTS OF SPEECH 3 • NOUNS AND PRONOUNS 5

FIND THAT VERB! 8 • LINKING VERBS 12 • AUXILIARY VERBS 13

ADJECTIVES 14 • ADJECTIVES' POSITION 16

ADJECTIVES FOR STYLE 16 • ADVERBS 18

ON TO PREPOSITIONS 19 • FINAL PREPOSITIONS 22

IN OR ON? 23 • COMMAS AND CONJUNCTIONS 24

CORRELATIVE AND ADVERBIAL CONJUNCTIONS 25

SUBORDINATING CONJUNCTIONS 27 • CLAUSES AND COMMAS 28

INTERJECTIONS 29 • SUBJECT-VERB AGREEMENT 29

EITHER AND NEITHER 38 • A QUESTION OF NUMBERS 39

AGREEMENTS WITH WHICH AND THAT 39

SENTENCE INTERRUPTERS 40

SUBJECT AND SUBJECT COMPLEMENT 41

TO SPLIT OR NOT TO SPLIT 42

ONLY AND JUST 44 • NONSEXIST PRONOUNS 46

SIMPLE PAST OR PRESENT PERFECT? 48 • WILL OR SHALL? 48

THE BURNT PROBLEM 49 • THE SUBJUNCTIVE 49

ACTIVE OR PASSIVE VOICE? 52

SECTION TWO:
IN WHICH DR. GRAMMAR ANSWERS QUESTIONS ABOUT USAGE
55

ITS OR IT'S? 58 • WHOSE OR WHO'S? 59

THEIR, THEY'RE, OR THERE? 59 • YOUR OR YOU'RE? 60

TO, TOO, OR TWO? 61 • CITE, SITE, OR SIGHT? 62

PASSED OR PAST? 63 • COURSE OR COARSE? 63

PLAIN OR PLANE? 64 • PEACE OR PIECE? 65

WEATHER OR WHETHER? 65 • PRINCIPAL OR PRINCIPLE? 66

COMPLIMENT OR COMPLEMENT? 67 • ALREADY OR ALL READY? 68

ALTOGETHER OR ALL TOGETHER? 68 • AWHILE OR A WHILE? 69

BESIDE OR BESIDES? 70 • EVERYDAY OR EVERY DAY? 70

CAN OR MAY? 71 • ACCEPT OR EXCEPT? 72

ADOPT OR ADAPT? 72 • ADVICE OR ADVISE? 73

AFFECT OR EFFECT? 73

CONTINUAL OR CONTINUOUS? 74 • APPRAISE OR APPRISE? 75

COMPRISE OR COMPOSE? 76 • CONSCIOUS OR CONSCIENCE? 77

SENSUAL OR SENSUOUS? 77 • EXPLICIT OR IMPLICIT? 78

INFER OR IMPLY? 78 • FEW OR LESS? 79 • LIKE OR AS? 80

ANXIOUS OR EAGER? 80 • JEALOUSY OR ENVY? 81

FARTHER OR FURTHER? 82 • AMOUNT OR NUMBER? 82

BRING OR TAKE? 83 • PERCENT OR PERCENTAGE? 84

GRADUATION DILEMMA 84 • WHO WEDS WHOM? 85

IN BEHALF OR ON BEHALF? 85 • REPETITIOUS REDUNDANCIES 86

IMPACT: NOUN OR VERB? 88

CONTENTS

SECTION THREE:

IN WHICH DR. GRAMMAR ANSWERS QUESTIONS ABOUT MECHANICS

89

TITLES OF WORKS 92 • NAMES WITH TITLES 94

NAMES WITH DEGREES 95

PUNCTUATION WITH ABBREVIATIONS 96

ACRONYMS 97 • FIGURES OR WORDS? 98 • TIME OF DAY 100

PAGE REFERENCES: FIGURES OR WORDS? 101 • WORD DIVISION 101

USING HYPHENS 103 • HYPHENS FOR CLARITY 105

HYPHENS WITH NUMBERS 106 • HYPHENS: YES OR NO? 107

PROPER AND COMMON NOUNS 108 • CAPITALS: YES OR NO? 110

mother or Mother? 113 • aunt or Aunt? 114

POSSESSIVE WITH *s* 115 • POSSESSIVE OF PLURALS 116

FORMING THE POSSESSIVE 116 • ABBREVIATIONS 120

CONTENTS

SECTION FOUR:
IN WHICH DR. GRAMMAR ANSWERS QUESTIONS ABOUT PUNCTUATION
123

QUESTION MARK OR PERIOD? 125

INDIRECT AND DIRECT QUESTIONS 126

COMMAS WITH ADJECTIVES 127 • COMMAS WITH NAMES 129

COMMAS WITH RESTRICTIVE PHRASES 130 • THAT OR WHICH? 131

COMMAS IN DATES 133 • SERIAL COMMAS 134

COMMAS WITH ABBREVIATIONS 136 • COMMAS WITH NAMES 137

COMMAS WITH PREPOSITIONAL PHRASES 137

COMMAS: YES OR NO? 138 • COMMAS FOR CONTRAST 139

COMMA BEFORE AND 140 • COMMAS WITH TOO 142

COMMAS FOR CLARITY 143 • SUBJECTS, COMMAS, AND VERBS 144

COMMA BEFORE INC. 145 • THE SEMICOLON 145 • THE COLON 148

COLON WITH SALUTATION 149 • COLON WITH SUBTITLE 150

CAPITAL AFTER COLON 150 • PARENTHESES OR BRACKETS? 152

DASHES 154 • PERIODS AND QUOTATION MARKS 154

PUNCTUATION WITH QUOTATION MARKS (? AND !) 155

PUNCTUATION WITH QUOTATION MARKS (; AND :) 156

ELLIPSIS POINTS 157 • QUESTIONS WITHIN QUESTIONS 158

POSTSCRIPT
159

CONTENTS

INTRODUCTION

"There's a grammatical error on the moon!"

That's what a friend of mine said with some concern recently. The plaque left by the first astronauts to land on the moon reads:

> Here men came from the planet Earth
> first set foot on the moon
> July 1969 A.D.
> We came in peace for all mankind.

My friend continued, "It should have read 'A.D. July 1969.' The A.D. must always precede and never follow the date. Also, I would have capitalized 'moon.' After all, it is a place, just as Chicago is a place."

As much as I hate to destroy a good story, I had to assure my friend that there is, in fact, no grammatical error on the moon. Perhaps there is a mistake in mechanics, usage, punctuation, or even spelling, but the moon has no grammatical mistake on it. Yet my friend seemed not to be convinced; she continues to feel that the plaque is not written correctly and therefore is certain that it has to have something to do with grammar. It turns out that she is not alone. The "grammatical error" was mentioned in a national periodical and several of my students brought clippings to class to discuss with me.

But a mistake in writing is not always a mistake in grammar. The placement of A.D. and the capitalization of "moon" are not concerns of grammar at all. Most of the so-called mistakes in writing that American speakers and writers of English make are not grammatical mistakes at all. They are usually only mistakes in usage, punctuation, mechanics, and the like.

I run a grammar hot line, called The Write Line, at Oakton Community College in Des Plaines, Illinois, where I teach. People call me at all hours of the day and even into the night (I have an answering machine for that!) with their questions, and I try to provide the answers. Here are some of the questions that were asked just this last week:

- When I am writing a business letter, can I abbreviate the name of the state or must it be spelled out completely?

- I'm mailing wedding invitations and have two friends who have lived together for many years but are not married. How do I address the invitation to the two of them?

- I need to write a letter to the rector of my church. Do I write out the word *Reverend* in his title or do I abbreviate it *Rev.?*

- My boss wants me to screen calls for him. Is there a polite way for me to find out who is calling without asking directly?

These were all interesting calls, and I answered each of them. But not one of these calls was about grammar. No matter what the caller might have done in any of these situations, the result would not be judged either grammatically correct or incorrect.

What, then, *is* grammar? And what constitutes a mistake in grammar? When most people think about grammar, they are thinking about what I call "language etiquette." More often than not, it involves the "print code." For instance, the placing of certain punctuation marks inside or outside quotation marks isn't a matter of grammar. Yes, I know that someone will insist that it is wrong to write *"I want to go home"*. Yes, it *is* wrong, but the error lies in the realm of the "print code"—the code of etiquette we all use when we print or write something. The sentence *"I want to go home"*. is grammatically correct. It is wrong or inappropriate only in so far as we agree that the period is always placed inside the quotation marks, not outside.

I've heard people insist that the sentence *I ain't done yet* is grammatically incorrect. The word *ain't* may be incorrect in certain situations, but whatever that situation might be, the sentence is not grammatically incorrect. Of course, in a formal or even semiformal situation, *ain't* is regarded as inappropriate language etiquette. Think of it as being similar to going to church dressed in a tank top, something that would usually be regarded as a violation of the dress-code etiquette for that time and place. I would not use *ain't* in formal writing or speaking. I might even raise some eyebrows using *done* in the sentence *I ain't done yet.* Nevertheless, *I ain't done yet* is *grammatically* correct.

Grammar is concerned with the form and structure of words and their relationships in phrases, clauses, and sentences. The difference between the sentences *John loves Mary* and *Mary loves John* is a matter of grammar. The entire meaning changes with the changing of word order in the sentences. Word order is one of the most significant concerns of grammar when we use the word *grammar* in its true sense. In terms of word order, most native speakers of English would not write *Eugene the ball threw Elise.* Even without knowing the names of the parts of language, the native speaker would put the words in their usual order and write *Eugene threw Elise the ball.*

In some languages, word order is not all that important. Let me go back to English's Latin roots to illustrate this, because most of our traditional rules in English come from Latin. Word order in Latin isn't as important. The sentence *John loves Mary* written in Latin is *Joannes Mariam amat,* the verb, as usual, coming at the end of the sentence. However, I can retain the same word order and the same basic words and change the meaning: *Joannem Maria amat.* This sentence translates to *Mary loves John.* The word order is the same, but the meaning changes. How? Notice the endings on the Latin for John and Mary: Maria/Mariam and Joannes/Joannem. These endings, called inflections, tell the reader which is the subject and which is the object of the verb *amat.*

These endings are another concern of grammar. English once had many more inflections than it has now. With regard to nouns, the basic inflections involve the singular and the plural: chair/chairs, hero/heroes, country/countries, shelf/

shelves. With pronouns, it's number and case (subject of a verb, object of a verb or preposition, or possession): I/we, he or she/they (number); I/me, I/my, she/her (case).

☞ Give the keys to *her.*
☞ *My* father is visiting from Kansas City.

It would be ungrammatical to write:

✗ Give the keys to *she.*
✗ *Me* father is visiting from Kansas City.

But as I wrote earlier, most native speakers of English would not make these errors. Most people are simply better grammarians—when the term is correctly understood—than they think. Without being consciously aware of it, people pick up the generally accepted patterns for word order and inflection that are a part of our collective grammar.

Grammar also deals with the form of words—even though the dictionary meanings are relatively or even exactly the same. *Bill's friendly song* is grammatically different from *Bill's friend sang,* but the dictionary meanings of those three words are basically the same. Because of the difference in the *form* of the words—adverb versus noun in *friendly/ friend* and noun versus verb in *song/sang*—we have two different grammatical structures and two totally different meanings.

Finally, if we take into account the spoken variety of English, and there are those who argue that spoken English takes precedence over written English, we have an additional structural device that lies within the purview of grammar. In spoken English we might call it intonation or stress; in written English it is called juncture and is signaled through punctuation.

☞ Alex the barber canceled my appointment.
☞ Alex, the barber canceled my appointment.

These two sentences are grammatically identical: The dictionary meanings of the words are the same, the order of the words is the same, as are the inflections and forms. Yet the placement of just one comma signals an entirely different meaning. In speaking, you would probably intonate or stress the word *Alex* and probably pause after saying his name. In writing, you indicate that you are speaking directly to Alex by placing a comma after the name. The difference in the two sentences has been made obvious by something so small as a single comma. In the first sentence, the barber's name is Alex, and you are stating that he canceled your appointment. In the second, you are addressing a person named Alex and stating that a barber, who is nameless in your sentence, canceled your appointment. Punctuation, in this case, becomes a grammatical element and a very important vehicle for conveying accurate meaning in your writing.

In the years that "Dr. Grammar" has been operating The Write Line at Oakton Community College, I have had very few calls with reference to "grammar" of this nature. Occasionally, I'll get something of the "Is it *John and me went to the ball game* or *John and I went . . . ?*" variety, or *Give a copy of the report to Sarah and I.* But the inquirers in these cases, I believe, are not ignorant of grammar; they are simply overcompensating. They are confused, and the confusion probably stems from the old mandates about *It's me* and *It's I.*

Most of the calls I receive are about usage, punctuation, mechanics, and spelling. More often than not, the callers are aware of options, and they are calling me just to double-check. Very often, the callers are secretaries questioning something their bosses dictated that just didn't look or sound right, calls about forms of address in the salutation of a letter to an official ("How does one address the pope in a letter?"), calls about the difference in meaning between jealousy and envy, or between precipitation and rain. (A lovely-sounding elderly lady once asked me to give her a list of "big" words to use in conversation with her son-in-law, whom she found intellectually intimidating. "What sort of words?" I asked. "Oh, just any that I can throw in now and then," she replied. Of course, I have also had my share of calls about the difference between *lie* and *lay*.

Before I get on to answering more pressing questions, let me leave you with this little scenario:

— *(Telephone: Ring, ring, ring)*
— Good afternoon. Oakton Community College. The Write Line. May I help you?
— Uh, yes. Is this the grammar hot line? Are you Dr. Grammar?
— Yes, it is, and yes, I am.
— I, uh, I, um, I have a question.
— Okay. How may I help you?
— My wife tells me that there is a difference between *shall* and *will.* Is that so? I seem to remember something about that, but neither one of us can remember the rule. Is there a difference?
— Yes, there is, or I should say there *was* a difference. It still exists, I suppose, but current usage doesn't demand

the distinction. Most people use *will* in preference to *shall*. To say or write *I shall go* sounds pretentious or affected today, especially in informal usage.

— Oh, so it's okay to use *will,* no matter what?

— Well, I'm not certain about the "no matter what" part, but you would be grammatically correct today to use *will* in most statements where you would also consider using *shall.* However, in questions involving *I* or *we,* you should use *shall,* as in "Shall I call you tomorrow?" or "Shall we go?" meaning "Are you ready to go?"

— Oh, I see. *(Pause)* But you said there is, or was, a distinction. Could you tell me about it?

— Certainly. It's somewhat of a complicated mess, but here goes. With the first person, *shall* indicates the future, as in "I shall go shopping," meaning that later today or tomorrow, or whenever, I am going to go shopping. With the second and third person, *shall* means determination. "You *shall* do it," or "He *shall* not come here!" Are you with me so far? Am I making this clear?

— Fine, so far. I think I've got it.

— Good. But here's the catch with *will.* With the first person, *will* means determination, as in "I will do it," meaning "I am determined to do it." The question of time is not an issue. But with the second and the third persons, *will* means simple future: "They *will* leave tomorrow" or "You *will* ask her tomorrow." As you can see, it is a fairly cumbersome distinction, and current usage allows you to use *will* with any person to indicate the future. Of course, I don't mean to tell you not to use *shall* or not to make that distinction if you want to. I still like to do so.

— Well, let me ask you just one more question.

— All right.

— You mentioned all that about "persons." The person determines the difference in meaning between *shall* and *will.* Right?

— Right.

— Okay, but I'm just a bit confused. *(Pause)* When do you start counting?

— Counting?

— *(Pause)* Yeah, do you do it every day . . . uh, or at a given time . . . or in a particular situation?

— *(Silence at my end this time . . . suddenly the proverbial light bulb goes on over my head. . . . I cover the mouthpiece . . .)*

— I mean, how does the person know if he is . . .

— Okay, sir, let me backtrack just a bit. The grammatical concept of first, second, or third person has nothing to do with . . . .

One of my favorite quotations—I use it all the time—is from Oliver Wendell Holmes, who gets my vote as the greatest jurist in American history. He said, "A word is the skin of a living thought." Only when words are used properly and the grammar is correct can you be certain that you are communicating your real message to your readers.

The Aztecs were right: He who speaks well gets to speak with the gods. Dr. Grammar likes to think that those who write well just might be able to write to the gods.

DR. GRAMMAR'S
WRITES
FROM
WRONGS

SECTION ONE:

IN WHICH DR. GRAMMAR

ANSWERS QUESTIONS

ABOUT GRAMMAR

Grammar, which knows how to control even kings.

—Molière, *Les Femmes Savantes*

QUESTION: My son, who is in the tenth grade, tells me that his teacher says that knowing the parts of speech is not important anymore. He certainly doesn't seem to know very much about them. When I was in school, we seemed to spend a lot of time studying the parts of speech. Don't they do that anymore? Aren't the parts of speech really important?

DR. GRAMMAR: It sounds to me as though you and I grew up in the same era, for I, too, certainly remember endless drills requiring me to label the various parts of speech. The problem we now recognize with those drills is that the knowledge did not necessarily transfer to good or even correct writing. Don't you remember sometimes doing especially well on a test on parts of speech and then getting a lower grade on a theme you wrote? I know I certainly do.

What we have come to realize in recent years is that knowing the parts of speech in a specific instance might be useful information, but it is not necessarily going to make you a competent writer. Remember that there is a major difference between being competent and being correct. A competent writer will, for the most part, be correct. A correct writer is not necessarily competent or, for that matter, even interesting.

The major problem with studying the parts of speech is that they have meaning only within the context of a single sentence. In any given sentence, each word has a function and can be labeled with one of the parts of speech—*noun, pronoun, verb, adjective, adverb, preposition, conjunction,* or *interjection.* But if that same word were used in a different sentence, it might receive an entirely different label. Here's a simple example:

☞ Alex has a dirty *face.* [*Face* is a noun telling what Alex has.]

☞ It is time that you *face* the music. [Here, the same word, *face,* spelled exactly the same way, is used as a verb.]

You can see from this example that it is wrong to say categorically that *face* is only a noun or that it is only a verb. *Face* functions as a noun or a verb depending on the specific sentence. When you say that any given word is a particular part of speech, you are only describing how it functions in a particular sentence, not how it will always function in the future.

★

QUESTION: I still have a problem shifting between nouns and pronouns, especially knowing which pronouns to use. Do you have a solution?

DR. GRAMMAR: First, let's review the function that a noun fulfills in a sentence. A *noun* is a word that names a person, a place, a thing, an idea, or an action. When you use it to name a specific person, place, or thing, you always capitalize it. If it names a general group or a class, or an idea or an action, you do not capitalize it unless it is the first word in the sentence. (For more about how to capitalize nouns, see pages 108–114.)

Persons:

☞ *Ralph* introduced *Mary* to his mother.

☞ *Professor Jones* teaches my cousin *Roger*.

Places:

☞ Our family home is in *New York*.

☞ The big lake is in the *valley*.

Things:

☞ My *car* has a broken *axle*.

☞ His *speech* took an interesting *position*.

Ideas:

☞ *Love* is the basis upon which *dreams* often rest.

☞ The *medium* is the *message*.

Actions:

☞ *To talk* about anything and everything was clearly his favorite hobby.

☞ *Running* is good exercise.

A pronoun is a word that takes the place of a noun in a sentence. In the sentence *Richard introduced Louise to Uncle John,* all of the nouns could be replaced by pronouns:

☞ *He* introduced Louise to Uncle John.
☞ Richard introduced *her* to Uncle John.
☞ Richard introduced Louise to *him.*
☞ *He* introduced *her* to *him.*

Depending on previous knowledge, the reader *must* know who is who.

If you really want to master pronouns, you will need some information about the different kinds of pronouns that are available.

1. *Personal pronouns* function as nouns when they name the person doing the speaking, the person being spoken to, or the person or thing being spoken about. Pronouns are different from nouns, however, because they change form according to whether they are used as subjects or objects. The following table will help you understand personal pronouns. The possessive pronouns that are in italics function as nouns. The other possessive pronouns serve as adjectives. I have included them here for you to see the various forms of the personal pronouns.

Number	Person	Subject	Object	Possession
Singular	1st person, speaker	I	me	my, *mine*
	2nd person, the person spoken to	you	you	your, *yours*
	3rd person, the person spoken of	he she it	him her it	his, *his* her, *hers* its
Plural	1st person, the speaker	we	us	our, *ours*
	2nd person, the person spoken to	you	you	your, *yours*
	3rd person, the person spoken of	they	them	their, *theirs*

2. A second kind of pronoun is the *interrogative pronoun*. It is used as a noun in asking questions. The interrogative pronouns are *who, which, what, whose,* and *whom.*

☞ *Who* is your gorgeous friend?
☞ *Which* of the stereo sets do you want?
☞ You did *what?*

3. You may remember from school that the *demonstrative pronouns—this, that, these, those—*are the ones that demonstrate or point out. They are the ones that are very useful when you want to be certain your reader knows exactly what you mean.

> ☞ *That* is the way I wish I could afford to dress.
> ☞ My father gave me *these* as a birthday present.
> ☞ *Those* are the books you should have given away.

4. And, finally, there are the *indefinite pronouns*. They are called indefinite because they do not refer to any specific person, place, or thing. They are not even automatically singular or plural. They really are indefinite. They take on their meaning from the context in which they are used. Typical indefinite pronouns are *one, someone, everybody, nobody, everybody, several, all, neither,* and *either.*

> ☞ *One* really has to have two jobs to survive today.
> ☞ *Someone* surely must know the author of that poem.
> ☞ He gives good grades to *everybody.*
> ☞ *All* are invited to my home.

★

QUESTION: How can I check a sentence and pinpoint the verb, and how do I know it is used correctly?

DR. GRAMMAR: I am sure you will understand verbs better if I review with you some of the main functions of the verb in a sentence.

The most common function a verb performs in a sentence is to express action:

☞ I *run* an hour every morning before breakfast.
☞ He *drove* madly along the freeway.
☞ We *played* football until it was too dark to see.

A verb can also express a state of being:

☞ She *remained* in her room all day.
☞ Alan *was* very happy to receive the news.

A verb can help to state a question:

☞ *Is* Robert the best worker in your office?
☞ *Did* you *put* the computer manual on the shelf?

A verb may express a command:

☞ *Sit* in the corner of the room.
☞ *Leave* through the side door.

Once you get the feel as to how verbs work in sentences, you can then use any of a series of four different tests to see if a particular word is indeed a verb.

a. Can you use the word as an infinitive, that is, can you put *to* in front of it? If you can, and the word still makes sense in the sentence, it is probably a verb.

Verb	*Not a Verb*
to sing	to circus
to play	to alone

b. If you can put *he* or *they* before the word and it makes sense, the word is a verb.

Verb	**Not a Verb**
He laughs.	He cheerfuls.
They dance.	They gorgeous.

c. Does the word have an *-ing* form? All verbs do.

Verb	**Not a Verb**
sing/singing	good/gooding
run/running	theater/theatering

d. Another method for identifying verbs is to see if the word comes in the most common "verb position" in the sentence. The typical sentence pattern in English is *noun + verb + complement* or *direct object.* Does the word in question come immediately after a noun that might also be the subject of the sentence?

Here is a nonsense sentence, but Dr. Grammar would bet that you can spot the verb anyway.

☞ E vlob repted u mismus virfly.

Remember what you already know about the grammar of a sentence:

- A noun is often preceded by a noun determiner, that is, a word like *a* or *the*. Doesn't *E* look like a good noun determiner? If this is true, *u* might also be a noun determiner. In this sentence you now can check for the following pattern: Noun determiner + noun + *repted* + noun determiner + noun + *virfly*.

- A verb typically follows a noun in the sentence, and many verbs end with *ed*. Try the pattern again: Noun determiner + noun + verb + noun determiner + noun + *virfly*.

- Adverbs often come after a verb and frequently end with *ly*. Try the pattern a final time: Noun determiner + noun + verb + noun determiner + noun + adverb.

See if you can make a sentence that will make sense by using the same pattern.

☞ The man raked the lawn gently.

Here is another nonsense pattern for guidance.

☞ U gflax barped e knert.

- What is the verb? How do you know?

- What is the subject? How do you know?

- What kind of word is *knert?* How do you know?

From this little exercise, you can readily see that it is the position in the sentence that determines the part of speech. You can also see that you have other structural signs within the structural pattern of the sentence that help you find its parts.

You should remember that only verbs can occupy the "verb position" in a sentence.

☞ You *call* us tomorrow morning.
☞ Alfredo *bought* the car just yesterday.
☞ The weather *is* so hot I can hardly stand it.

★

QUESTION: Last night, my daughter asked me to help her with her homework, and I got stuck. She was doing an exercise that asked her to identify linking verbs. The only words I remember from my own schoolwork that fit this category are words like *is* and *was.* What is a linking verb? Surely there are more of them than I could think of last night.

DR. GRAMMAR: You were right in remembering that forms of the verb *to be (is, am, are, was, were, be, being,* and *been*) are linking verbs. And, yes, there are others, too. A *linking verb* is one that does not express action. Instead, it describes a state of being or existence. The linking verb literally *links* the subject to the word or words that follow it.

☞ Don *is* my secretary.
☞ The children *were* quiet all during church.
☞ My sister *had been* to the museum before.

In addition to *to be,* other common linking verbs are *become, appear, remain, seem, taste, sound, smell,* and *feel.*

☞ The fried chicken *tasted* delicious.
☞ The surgeon *remained* calm during the operation.
☞ I thought the winter wind *felt* good.

LINKING VERBS

12

If you have a question about whether one of these verbs is a linking verb, try to substitute a form of *to be* for it. If that works, you have a true linking verb.

☞ The fried chicken *is* delicious.
☞ The surgeon *was* calm during the operation.
☞ I thought the winter wind *was* good.

The linking verb may link the subject with a word that actually restates (or renames) the subject. Do you remember something from high school called the *predicate noun?*

☞ *Greg* is the *usher.*
☞ My favorite *food* is *fish.*

With both of these, notice that you could just as easily turn the sentence around:

☞ The *usher* is *Greg.*
☞ *Fish* is my favorite *food.*

The linking verb may also link the subject with an adjective that describes the subject but cannot take the place of the subject. These, remember, are called *predicate adjectives.*

☞ The floral *arrangement* is absolutely *stunning.*
☞ His new *cologne* smelled *terrible.*

★

QUESTION: Are helping verbs and auxiliary verbs the same?

DR. GRAMMAR: You use *auxiliary verbs* to *help* make the necessary tense forms of other verbs. Think for a moment about how the typical auxiliary (or helping) verbs—*be, have, had, can, could, may, might, shall, should, will,* and *would*—change the tense of the verbs they are used with:

☞ I *can see* (present tense)
☞ I *will see* (future tense)
☞ I *had seen* (past perfect tense)

Look how the meanings of these sentences change with the changing of auxiliary verbs:

☞ The players *had performed* their best.
☞ The players *will perform* their best.
☞ The players *could perform* their best.
☞ The players *might have performed* their best.
☞ The players *would have performed* their best.

★

QUESTION: What is the role of adjectives in a sentence? Is there a special place where they have to go, or can they go anywhere?

DR. GRAMMAR: *Adjectives* are used to modify nouns or pronouns by limiting or describing them. They usually tell *which one, what kind,* or *how many.* Single-word adjectives always come in front of the noun they modify.

The most common adjectives are the articles *a, an,* and *the.* They help to answer the question *which one.*

☞ Fred read *a* book during his vacation in Hawaii.
☞ Susan took *the* report and gave it to her supervisor.

Other typical adjectives that answer the *which one* question include *every, each,* and *any.*

☞ Give *every* person in the room ten dollars.
☞ I put *each* nut and bolt into that cabinet myself.
☞ Is there *any* person here who needs help with the form?

Then, too, there are certain pronoun and noun forms that are used as adjectives when they answer the *which one* question.

☞ I think I have found *his* car keys.
☞ Did you drive by *Christine's* house?
☞ We saw *that* man in the neighborhood last night.

Other adjectives answer the question *how many.* Notice that these adjectives do not always have to be "number" words.

☞ We have *three* hours before our plane leaves.
☞ I heard that there were *many* people at the ball game last night.
☞ Amy saw *several* of her friends from high school.
☞ I can't think of *one* thing I like about that little grocery store on the corner.

Most adjectives answer the question *what kind.*

☞ My aunt has a *silver* tea set.
☞ The *barking* dog kept me awake all night.
☞ Harold bought one of those *cheap imported* cars.

QUESTION: Where do adjectives go in a sentence? I know that in some of the places where I try to put them they don't look right, but I don't know exactly what is wrong.

DR. GRAMMAR: Single adjectives, even if there are several of them back to back, should be placed immediately in front of the noun they modify.

> ☞ *The blue* car is still sitting beside the road.
> ☞ *The wrecked blue* car is still sitting beside the road.
> ☞ *The old wrecked blue* car is still sitting beside the road.

On the other hand, adjectival phrases and clauses are usually placed immediately after the noun they modify.

> ☞ Hand me the report *that is on Jean's desk.*
> ☞ The book *on the kitchen table* must be returned to the library.
> ☞ The person *who called you yesterday* is on the phone again this morning.

★

QUESTION: I have a friend who writes extremely well, and it seems to me he always does fresh things with his word placement. Can words be moved around in the sentence to give a better stylistic effect?

DR. GRAMMAR: Yes, you can move certain words around in a way that gives the sentence a fresh sound and that may even direct special attention to the word or words that you move. But you should never put a single adjective immediately after the noun it modifies. Do not say, for instance, *The dog old lay sleeping on the rug.* But see the flexibility possible if you have two adjectives that can be paired as modifiers of the same noun. The conventional sentence would look something like this:

☞ The *tired old* dog lay sleeping on the rug.

You could put the adjectives *tired* and *old* into a clause and write:

☞ The dog, which was *tired and old,* lay sleeping on the rug.

Or you could achieve an even more effective style by writing the sentence like this:

☞ The dog, *tired and old,* lay sleeping on the floor.

Here is another example that shows you the different effects you can get by moving adjectives around in the sentence:

☞ The *interesting but frightening* novel continues to occupy my mind.
☞ The novel, *which is interesting but frightening,* continues to occupy my mind.
☞ The novel, *interesting but frightening,* continues to occupy my mind.
☞ *Interesting but frightening,* the novel continues to occupy my mind.

Just remember that you must keep the adjective in close relationship to the noun it modifies; in the above example, to *novel*. If you wrote *The novel continues to occupy my mind, interesting but frightening,* you would be putting the adjectives next to *mind* and saying that your mind, not the novel, was interesting but frightening. Adjectives can be fun to move around for stylistic effect, but be careful that they remain close to the nouns they are intended to modify.

★

QUESTION: Doesn't the adverb really have a lot more usefulness in the sentence than the adjective? Can't it be placed almost anywhere in the sentence?

DR. GRAMMAR: An *adverb* can be used to modify a verb, an adjective, or even another adverb.

☞ Modifies a verb: The car ran *smoothly.*
☞ Modifies an adjective: You have a *very* attractive home.
☞ Modifies an adverb: She speaks *so* softly that I can hardly hear her.

Adverbs typically answer such questions as *where, when, how,* and *to what extent.*

☞ Where: Park your car *here.*
☞ When: I will call you *tomorrow.*
☞ How: We won the game *easily.*
☞ To what extent: She was *terribly* embarrassed.

When an adverb modifies an adjective or another adverb, it usually comes immediately before the word it modifies.

☞ Arthur was *very* unhappy with the decision.
☞ We had an *extremely* unpleasant evening.
☞ The new supervisor seemed *unusually* friendly.

When an adverb modifies the verb, it can occur almost anywhere in the sentence. But be aware that the mood of the sentence can shift when you move the adverb around.

☞ *Slowly* we began to learn Russian.
☞ We *slowly* began to learn Russian.
☞ We began *slowly* to learn Russian.
☞ We began to learn Russian *slowly*.

★

QUESTION: Why does English have so many different prepositions? What is their function in a sentence?

DR. GRAMMAR: We do, indeed, have a large number of prepositions, and Dr. Grammar admits that it is sometimes difficult to know which one to use in a given instance. Let me see if I can clarify the matter.

A *preposition* is used before a noun or a pronoun (called the *object of the preposition*) to form a phrase. A prepositional phrase usually limits or makes more exact the meaning of another word in the sentence. Look at these short examples:

☞ Douglas sat quietly *on the flagpole*.
☞ Douglas ran *around the swimming pool* three times.
☞ Douglas hid the camera *beneath the picnic basket*.
☞ Douglas put his coat *over his shoulders*.
☞ Douglas talked *in an excited voice*.

Remember that prepositions require objects. In order to determine if a word is a preposition, look to see if it is followed by an object, something that will answer the question *what* after the preposition. If you look at the "Douglas" examples above, you can see how the object does indeed answer the *what*s.

on what?	flagpole
around what?	pool
beneath what?	basket
over what?	shoulders
in what?	voice

If the object is a pronoun, you have to be certain that you use the objective-case form of the pronoun (see page 6). These forms, once again, are *me, you, him, her, it, them,* or *whom.*

☞ Jim gave *her* his notebook.
☞ Elaine asked Todd and *me* to his party.

Prepositions are very often words that show direction or motion. Years ago, it became popular for a teacher to draw a huge house on the blackboard and to tell students that any word they could put in physical relationship to that house— words such as *under, on, around, toward, from, into, above*—was a preposition. This technique may be a bit too simplified, but it is a good one to keep in mind if you want to remember what a preposition is and how it functions.

Here is a list of some of the most commonly used prepositions:

about	beside	into	through
above	between	like	throughout
according to	beyond	near	till
across	by	next to	to
after	concerning	of	toward
against	contrary to	off	under
along	despite	on	underneath
amid	down	onto	until
among	during	over	unto
around	for	past	up
aside	from	regarding	upon
at	in	regardless of	with
before	including	relative to	within
behind	inside	respective	without
below	instead of	round	
beneath		since	

Remember, though, what I said at the beginning of this section: *No word is automatically a specific part of speech.* How a word is labeled depends on how it functions in a certain sentence. Look at the word *across* in these two sentences:

☞ I looked *across* the aisle to see if you were watching. [The word *aisle* answers the *what* question after *across,* so *across* functions as a preposition in this example.]

☞ I looked *across* to see if you were watching. [Nothing answers *what* after *across* in this example, so *across* cannot be a preposition. It is actually an adverb here, simply reporting where I looked.]

★

QUESTION: What do you think about ending a sentence with a preposition? Are grammarians as fussy about this as they used to be?

DR. GRAMMAR: As I explained in the response to the previous question, a preposition must have an object. If a word that looks like a preposition appears at the end of a sentence but does not have an object following it that answers the question *what,* traditionalists believe the sentence should be recast. As a careful writer, you are wise not to make a habit of ending your sentences with prepositions. Keep in mind that your reader is used to hearing an object announced after such words as *to, from,* and *for.* Based on this practice, the reader wants to know *to what, from what,* or *for what.* When you don't answer such questions for your reader, you call attention to a change from the expected. At certain times this may, indeed, be something you want to do.

Dr. Grammar notes that some ideas simply lend themselves to ending with a word that looks like a preposition but which may be functioning merely as an adverb (see the examples with *across* on page 21). Don't force the sentence into an awkward construction. There is nothing at all incorrect with sentences like these:

☞ Have you already turned your report *in?*
☞ Please put the coat *on.*
☞ Before you begin the test, you must put your books *down.*

★

QUESTION: I've been in this country only three years and I'm still having trouble with the language. I never know if I should say *in* or *on*. Do I say *I got in the plane?* or *I got on the plane?*

DR. GRAMMAR: Dr. Grammar congratulates you. If this is the biggest problem you are having with English after being here for only three years, you have done exceedingly well. The problem you are describing is actually one that involves the use of prepositions in certain parts of our language, and, quite frankly, it does get confusing. The *in/on* problem that you describe is a good example. For the most part, we use *in* if we get completely inside something, if we are surrounded top and bottom.

☞ I got *in* the car. [You are completely surrounded by the car.]

And we typically use *on* for situations where we are not completely surrounded.

☞ He sat *on* the desk. [He is not surrounded by the desk but merely sitting on top of it.]

☞ We finally got *on* our bicycles and began the trip. [Again, a bicycle doesn't completely surround you.]

This guideline is generally followed, but you will find exceptions. Look at this typical expression:

☞ We got *on* the plane and flew to London. [Dr. Grammar certainly hopes that you are surrounded by the plane in this instance.]

The preceding sentence is a good example of the *idiomatic* way we use language. It may have no logical explanation; it is just the way it is most often said. The best way to pick up idiomatic expressions is to become a good listener, then use the language patterns that you hear frequently.

★

QUESTION: Yesterday at work I was arguing with my office friend about a sentence. She had used a comma; I thought she needed a semicolon. I knew I was right, but I couldn't explain my position very well. I think that the correct choice had to do with the difference between what I remember as a coordinating conjunction and a subordinating conjunction, but it has been fifteen years since I was in school and I'm not certain anymore. Do these two kinds of conjunctions determine whether you need a comma or a semicolon in the sentence?

DR. GRAMMAR: Many of the problems concerning commas and/or semicolons for separating sentence parts are related directly to the kind of conjunction that is used to join the parts. Let me explain this by using the easiest type of conjunction first and we'll see the different roles they play in sentences.

The simplest of all conjunctions is the *coordinating conjunction.* It is used to join words, phrases, and sentences that are of equal value.

☞ Pretza *and* Herr Schmitz are my dogs.
☞ Thinking on his feet *and* speaking directly to the issue are certainly his strong points.

COMMAS AND CONJUNCTIONS

☞ You may go to the movie with us *or* you may stay at home by yourself.

The principal coordinating conjunctions are *and, but, or,* and *nor.* The coordinating conjunction can join two independent clauses, clauses that can stand on their own as complete sentences. When the conjunction is used in this manner, it is preceded by a comma unless the two clauses are extremely short.

☞ Jayne wants to go into town tomorrow morning, *and* she has asked that you meet her for lunch at Ziro's.

☞ The report was ready to be mailed early this morning, *but* no one could find the right address for the envelope.

☞ I'm going to the zoo tomorrow *and* I hope you will go with me. [Because this sentence is so short, you don't have to put a comma before *and.* But my advice, though, is not to worry about it; go ahead and put one in if it feels right to you. The sentence would be considered correct with or without the comma.]

★

QUESTION: Well, then, what is a correlative conjunction and how is it used in writing? Must we always use a comma with it?

DR. GRAMMAR: *Correlative conjunctions* are somewhat like coordinating conjunctions in that they are used to join words or phrases of equal value. The major difference is that *correlative conjunctions* are always used in pairs. The most common pairs are *either-or, neither-nor, both-and,* and *not only-but also.* The correlative conjunction does not require special punctuation.

☞ I appreciated *both* the rhythm *and* the lyrics of that last song.

☞ *Either* John will present the facts at the meeting tomorrow *or* we will have to call in another consultant.

☞ Getting a good education is *not only* our responsibility *but also* our duty.

You should also know about the third kind of conjunction that is frequently used. It is called the *adverbial conjunction;* it is sometimes called the *conjunctive adverb.* This conjunction is used to join clauses of equal value. The most common conjunctions in this category are *however, consequently, therefore, accordingly, nevertheless, hence,* and *moreover.* This conjunction is usually preceded by a semicolon and followed by a comma.

☞ He had not studied for the test; *consequently,* he did poorly.

☞ It is one thing to believe strongly that you will be successful in life; *however,* it is helpful to work hard.

Sometimes the adverbial conjunction may be used at the beginning of a sentence for stylistic effect. Look at the difference in the following two sentences. They are identical except in the way they use the conjunction to create greater emphasis:

☞ The party was wild; *however,* I will never go there again.

☞ The party was wild. *However,* I will never go there again.

★

QUESTION: And what is a subordinating conjunction? I never seem to know what I am subordinating.

DR. GRAMMAR: The *subordinating conjunction* is used to join a subordinate (dependent) clause to a word or to another clause on which it depends. Some of the most common subordinating conjunctions are *although, because, since, then, if, that, unless, until, when, where,* and *while.* These conjunctions are called *subordinating* because they make the part of the sentence they introduce subordinate (dependent) upon something else. It's really very simple.

☞ The weather seems ideal. The fish are still not biting. [Two complete sentences, each standing alone.]

☞ *Although* the weather seems ideal, the fish are still not biting. [By introducing the first clause with a subordinating conjunction, you make it dependent upon the idea in the second clause for its meaning.]

☞ You should think about working overtime next week. You could certainly use the money.

☞ You should think about working overtime next week *because* you could certainly use the money.

★

QUESTION: Aren't clauses that are introduced by subordinating conjunctions set off from the rest of the sentence by commas?

DR. GRAMMAR: The subordinated clause is followed by a comma if it begins the sentence. No comma is needed if the clause comes later in the sentence.

A comma is needed in the following sentences:

☞ When I get up in the morning, I immediately brush my teeth.

☞ Unless Mark gets here very soon, we're going to have to leave without him.

☞ Until I read the assigned articles, I was utterly confused by his lecture.

No comma is needed in these sentences:

☞ I immediately brush my teeth when I get up in the morning.

☞ We're going to have to leave without Mark unless he gets here very soon.

☞ I was utterly confused by his lecture until I read the assigned articles.

For some reason, writers are tempted to put a comma in front of *because* when it introduces a subordinated clause at the end of the sentence. The guideline applies to *because,* as it does to all other subordinating conjunctions: Use a comma to separate the subordinated clause at the beginning of the sentence, but do not use a comma when the clause comes at the end.

Here, a comma is needed:

☞ Because she has studied hard, she is not at all worried about the test.

Here, no comma is needed:

☞ She is not worried about the test because she has studied hard.

★

QUESTION: What is an interjection and how do I employ it in a written sentence?

DR. GRAMMAR: An *interjection* is used to express a strong feeling or emotion. It has no grammatical relationship to the rest of the sentence. Because it is used to express emotion, it is commonly accompanied by the exclamation point. Remember, though, that when you use too many interjections or too many exclamation points, you weaken their effectiveness.

☞ Stop! I can't stand hearing you talk that way.
☞ Mercy! Is it really you?
☞ Heavens! I wish you had told me that last week.

★

QUESTION: I saw an advertisement on the back of a cereal box the other day that said, ". . . as nutritious as bread and butter is." *Is* doesn't sound right to me. Shouldn't it be *are?*

DR. GRAMMAR: You bring up a special case among the dozens of potential subject-and-verb agreement problems. Nouns and verbs can be either singular or plural, and most of the time we have no trouble with them. The basic rule is that the subject governs the verb; that is, if you have a singular subject, you must have a singular form of the verb (he/is); if you have a plural subject, you must use a plural form of the verb (they/are).

☞ Harold *is* waiting for you in the car.
☞ The children *are* waiting for you in the car.

When you have a compound subject—two or more subjects joined by a conjunction, usually *and*—the subject all but demands a plural form of the verb.

☞ Harold and Otis *are* waiting for you in the car.
☞ The wrecked car and the damaged fence *were* clear evidence of my need for driving lessons.

It is true, however, that certain words are used so often together that they have come to be regarded as a single unit rather than as two separate units. Such is the case with your particular concern. *Bread* and *butter* are not regarded as two separate things but as one thing: *bread and butter. Is* was the correct verb in the example.

Here are some more compound-subject examples. You will see that they usually come from food-related items that are typically consumed as a single unit:

☞ Gin and tonic *is* my favorite summer cocktail.

☞ Macaroni and cheese *is* one of my father's favorite dishes.

☞ Eggs and toast *was* always his favorite breakfast.

There may be times when you wish to emphasize the separate identities of the parts of a compound. You can do this by using a plural form of the verb.

☞ Both bread and butter *were* served at the banquet.

☞ Macaroni and cheese *are* only two of the ingredients in that recipe.

☞ Imported English dry gin and a good-quality tonic water *make* the best drink.

★

QUESTION: I remember studying *everyone, everybody, anyone,* and *anybody* in high school. Aren't these words called pronouns? Are they singular or plural? It seems to me that *everyone* is clearly singular and *everybody* is clearly plural. Am I on the right track?

DR. GRAMMAR: All aboard! You are talking about pronouns all right—*indefinite pronouns*. They are indefinite because they do not refer to specific people or things. That's the easy part. The confusing part comes when one starts trying to figure out whether they are singular or plural. Let's see how I can help.

These indefinite pronouns are always singular:

each	neither
every	one

everyone	anyone
everybody	anybody
nobody	someone
either	somebody

☞ *Neither is* a valid excuse.
☞ *Someone calls* every night about this time.
☞ *Somebody calls* every night about this time.

These indefinite pronouns are always plural:

both	several
many	few

☞ *Both are* good excuses.
☞ *Few were* able to complete the work on time.

But the following indefinite pronouns can be either singular or plural; it depends upon the noun in the phrase that comes immediately after them:

most	some
all	none
any	more

☞ *Most* of the students *are* attending the concert.
☞ *Most* of the work *has* been completed.

☞ *Some* of the messages *are* lost in the file.
☞ *Some* of the time *was* wasted.

☞ *All* of the children *are* asleep.

☞ *All* of the money *is* in the bank.

★

QUESTION: Is the sentence *Each of the students was awarded a diploma* correct? It seems to me that *students* is the subject and that the verb should be *were*, not *was*.

DR. GRAMMAR: You must not be misled by words that come between a subject and a verb. They do not affect the form of the verb. In your example, the word just before the verb is *students*, but *students* is not the subject of the sentence and it does not control the verb. *Each* is the subject of the sentence; think of the subject as singular—*each student*. *Students* is the object of the preposition *of*. You must be sure that you identify the subject of the sentence correctly.

☞ Six *pieces* of equipment *were* missing.

☞ *One* of my keys *is* lost somewhere.

☞ If *any* of the materials *was* lost, I am not going to assume responsibility.

★

QUESTION: Does the word *jury* take a singular or a plural noun?

DR. GRAMMAR: Words like *jury, committee,* and *fruit* are called *collective nouns* because they express the concept of group as a single whole; that is, they are collected. The people or objects are treated as a unit and are usually considered singular.

☞ The jury *continues* to debate the fate of Mr. A. K. Wilkins.

☞ The finance committee *meets* every Thursday afternoon.

☞ Meanwhile, the fruit *sits* rotting on the kitchen table.

There are times, however, when the individual members of the collective body act independently of one another. If you wish to give emphasis to that independent activity, you must use a verb in its plural form. It's all in the context, however, Look at these examples:

☞ The jury *is* being empaneled today. [Here, the jury is being used as a collective group.]

☞ The jury *are* divided nine to three on the credibility of Melissa's testimony. [The emphasis is on the quandary of the twelve individual members of the group.]

And these:

☞ The couple *is* being married today. [The couple here is one unit.]

☞ The couple *have* demanding jobs. [They are two people, both of whom have demanding jobs.]

☞ The faculty *meets* in the conference room. [The faculty as a collective group.]

☞ The faculty *have* written their reports on the problem. [The individual members of the faculty have written their separate reports.]

★

QUESTION: Should I write *The data has been collected* or *The data have been collected?* My boss and I are having a major argument about this.

DR. GRAMMAR: You must be especially careful with certain Latinate nouns. They may look singular and you may even see them used with a singular verb, but they are really plural and should always take a plural verb.

☞ The data *have been collected.*
☞ The criteria *were explained* by the judge.

But if you have only one piece of data or only one criterion, you of course must use a singular verb.

☞ The datum *was* misunderstood.
☞ Please state one criterion of what you consider to be an acceptable job.

★

QUESTION: When the name of a company is itself a possessive form, is it singular or plural? For example, is it correct to write *Macy's is having a sale,* or should it be *Macy's are having a sale?*

DR. GRAMMAR: Usage experts are in disagreement about this issue, and we also tend to disagree about the use of *they* when used to refer to a company. In general, these names are considered singular and therefore should take singular forms of a verb, and the company should be referred to by *it,* not *they.*

☞ Bloomingdale's *is* expanding *its* presence in the Midwest.

☞ Macy's *has* the best price on coats at *its* branch stores.

Incidentally, you should never use a second *'s* after a company name that is already possessive. Just the other day, Dr. Grammar read the sentence *A Bloomingdale's's charge card makes my life more fun.* There is no need for that extra *'s.* Write simply, *A Bloomingdale's charge card makes my life more fun.* (As indeed it does.)

★

QUESTION: At my office I write a lot of reports that contain money amounts, and I never know if I should make these singular or plural. Is it *$10,000 was spent* or *$10,000 were spent?*

DR. GRAMMAR: When an amount of money is the subject of a sentence, you should use the singular form of a verb when the figure represents the total amount of money.

☞ Fifty dollars *is* a lot of money for a child to carry to school.

☞ More than $10,000 *was* spent to remodel the office.

☞ I'm sorry, sir, but your six dollars *is* not refundable.

Each of these is seen as a total amount, not as individual dollar amounts. But if the amount represents individual dollar amounts, use a plural form of a verb.

☞ Hundreds of dollars *have* been wasted on the Huntley project.

☞ Ten more dollars *are* needed to pay for the cart.

★

QUESTION: When the subject of the sentence is *majority,* do I use the singular or the plural form of a verb?

DR. GRAMMAR: *Majority* falls into the same category as the indefinite pronouns discussed earlier (see page 31). It is neither singular nor plural by definition. Like indefinite pronouns, it is usually followed by an *of* clause. If the object of that *of* is singular, use the singular form of a verb; if it's plural, use the plural:

☞ The majority of time *was* spent discussing the new budget.

☞ The majority of votes *were* for the amendment.

The noun *part* works in exactly the same way:

☞ *Part* of the Tulsa staff *is* being transferred to St. Louis.

☞ *Part* of the executive suites *are* being remodeled.

These same guidelines, incidentally, apply to the times you use fractions (see page 106 for more on fractions) in your writing:

☞ Three fourths of our work *is* boring.
☞ Three fourths of the people *are* boring.

☞ Two thirds of the day *was* wasted.
☞ Two thirds of the leaves *have* fallen.

★

QUESTION: If the word *neither* is used with other nouns in a sentence, does that determine if the subject is singular or plural?

DR. GRAMMAR: No. *Neither* and *either* are always singular. Do not become confused if neither or either comes before a noun that is plural.

☞ Neither of the students *was* on time for class.
☞ Either Bill or Susan *has* to present the lecture.
☞ Neither of the two choices *was* acceptable to Professor Gray.

If *either* or *neither* comes before nouns joined by *or* or *nor,* you have to think a bit. In those instances, the verb agrees in number with the noun that is nearest to it.

☞ Either John or his cousins *are* planning to mow the lawn this afternoon.
☞ Neither his cousins nor John *is* planning to mow the lawn this afternoon.

The rule applies even if you do not have the word *either* or *neither* at the head of the sentence. If you have two (or more) subjects joined by *or* or *nor,* the verb always agrees in number with the one nearest to it.

☞ The dog or the cats *are* shedding all over the couch.

☞ The cats or the dog *is* in big trouble right now.

★

QUESTION: What is the difference between *a number* and *the number?* I seem to hear the two terms used interchangeably. Is there any distinction?

DR. GRAMMAR: There is indeed a distinction, and the two terms can't be used properly if you don't know what that distinction is. The term *the number* is always singular, and it always takes the singular form of a verb.

☞ The number of new employees *has* decreased this year.

☞ The number of suburban transit centers *is* expanding rapidly.

The term *a number* is plural and takes the plural form of a verb.

☞ A number of employees *have* already received a promotion.

☞ A number of suburban transit centers *are* outgrowing their original spaces.

★

QUESTION: I need help with the correct form of the verb to use after *which* or *that.* Singular or plural?

DR. GRAMMAR: The words *which* and *that* are adjective-clause signals. That is, they—as well as *who, whose,* and *whom*—are generally used to introduce adjective clauses. Because the pronouns themselves are neither singular nor plural, you must find the noun to which they refer and check if it is singular or plural, then use the form of the verb that agrees in number with that noun (the antecedent).

☞ I found the television set that *is* on sale.

☞ I found the television sets that *are* on sale.

☞ There will be a meeting with the salesman who *has* just returned from London.

☞ Reports from the salesmen who *have* been away are due tomorrow.

☞ Employees must sign for the key, which *is* in my office.

☞ Students must sign for the tools, which *are* in my studio.

★

QUESTION: This morning my boss gave me a report to type. One sentence says, *Each supervisor, along with his staff, is expected to be present for the entire training session.* That doesn't sound right to me. Because he is writing about both the supervisor *and* his staff, doesn't he need the plural verb *are* in the sentence?

DR. GRAMMAR: No, your boss happens to be correct. There are phrases in English that we call *sentence interrupters* because they seem to interrupt the flow of the sentence. These phrases are always set off from the rest of the sentence by commas, to show that they could be taken out of the sentence without damaging the meaning of the sentence. Other frequently used sentence-interrupter phrases are *along with, together with,* and *in addition to.*

☞ Alex, together with his three cousins from Detroit, *was* growing tired of seeing museums.

☞ Ms. Flavum, in addition to all of the other secretaries in her office, *has* complained about the poor ventilation.

★

QUESTION: I think I understand the principles of subject and verb agreement, but I still have a question. What happens in those instances where you have a sentence with a singular subject and a plural subject complement? With which does the verb agree?

DR. GRAMMAR: Those instances are rare, but they do occur. When they do, simply remember that the verb always agrees in number with the subject of the sentence, not with the complement.

☞ The important concern here *is* lower temperatures in the work environment. [The subject is the *concern,* not temperatures, so the singular form of the verb is needed.]

☞ Horses *are* her only love. [The subject is *horses,* not the love they inspire, so use the plural.]

★

QUESTION: What is the present thinking about splitting an infinitive? We were taught not to do it, but I see and hear it more and more lately. Is it now okay?

DR. GRAMMAR: Dr. Grammar finds nothing wrong with splitting an infinitive (as long as you don't say, "To be or to not be"). Remember that an *infinitive* is *to + verb,* such as to run, to talk, to play, etc., and that it functions in the sentence as a noun. Usage experts today see nothing at all incorrect with the split-infinitive structure.

☞ Alfredo wants *to quickly talk* with you about his new idea.

☞ Beth wants *to quietly play* some music at her desk while you work.

Although there is nothing wrong with the grammar that occurs when you split an infinitive with an adverb, there are times when you might create an awkward or even confusing structure by doing so. The problem, then, is more one of style than of grammar. The problem is especially true when *not* is the adverb:

x He decided only yesterday *to not go* on the geological expedition.

You will agree that that is an extremely awkward construction. Look how much smoother it is without the split infinitive:

☞ He decided only yesterday *not to go* on the geological expedition.

Here is another awkward sentence, this time with *even:*

✗   It was not possible *to even get* a phone interview.

Here it is without the split infinitive:

☞ It was not possible *even to get* a phone interview.

However, there are situations where you can be more exact by splitting the infinitive. Consider the construction that results when a writer places the adverb away from the infinitive it modifies.

✗   Mr. Edwards asked the staff *to review* the president's memorandum concerning the evacuation of the building *carefully.*

The intention was to have the staff *carefully review* the memo. The meaning would be much clearer if *carefully* were placed between *to* and *review*:

☞ Mr. Edwards asked the staff *to carefully review* the president's memorandum concerning the evacuation of the building.

Look at the ambiguity in this sentence:

✗   The committee decided immediately *to implement* the planned emergency procedures.

Did the committee *decide* immediately, or to *implement* immediately? One way the ambiguity can be resolved is by splitting the infinitive:

☞ The committee decided *to immediately implement* the planned emergency procedures.

★

QUESTION: Where did the rule to not split infinitives come from?

DR. GRAMMAR: I'll be glad to tell you, but first let me point out that Dr. Grammar caught you at your little trick. You are toying with me, aren't you? You ask about splitting an infinitive and then you do exactly that in your own question.

The rule, which Dr. Grammar feels is archaic and even silly, comes from Latin grammar. In classical Latin, it was not possible to split the infinitive because the infinitive structure was only one word and as such could not be split.

English infinitive structure	*Latin infinitive structure*
to love	amare
to praise	laudare
to move	movere
to sing	cantare

Our grammarian forefathers and foremothers simply carried over this Latin concept and applied it to English grammar, where it makes no sense at all.

★

QUESTION: I am often bothered by the way some people use the adverb *only*. They usually put it before the verb, where it gives a meaning they probably do not intend. Am

I right? Doesn't the word *only* have a special place in the sentence where it *should* be used?

DR. GRAMMAR: You are quite observant of our language. Yes, *only* (and *just,* too, for that matter) often gets misplaced in a sentence, leading to meanings that the writer probably did not intend. The word *only* should be placed before the word it modifies. Consider the following sentences:

☞ I *only* want two copies of the report.

☞ Helen *only* spoke for a short time.

In the first of the two sentences above, *only* modifies *want;* in the second, *spoke.* If this premise is true, the writer is saying in the first sentence, *I only want.* All I do all day long is want. I don't dream. I don't sleep. I don't work. I just want. The writer of the second sentence is saying that Helen never did anything except speak. She didn't dance, she didn't sing, she didn't whistle. *Helen only spoke.* If *only* is put before the words it modifies, the intended meaning of each sentence becomes clear.

☞ I want *only* two copies of the report. [You don't want sixteen copies.]

☞ Helen spoke for *only* a short time. [Helen didn't go on and on.]

Look at the difference in meaning between these two sentences:

☞ Dave *just* plays football.

☞ Dave plays *just* football.

In the first, the writer is saying that all Dave ever does is play football. In the second, the writer indicates that the only game in which Dave participates is football. Quite a difference! The placement of *only* can change the meaning of a sentence:

☞ *Only* Bill eats a small salad for dinner.
☞ Bill eats *only* a small salad for dinner.
☞ Bill eats a small salad *only* at dinner.

In the first sentence, *only* modifies Bill, thus revealing that while other people eat other foods, poor Bill makes do with just a small salad. The second sentence indicates that Bill's entire dinner consists solely of a small salad. The third sentence says that Bill eats a small salad only at dinner and at no other time.

Careful writers are very much aware of choices, and we all want to be careful, exact writers so that our words and therefore our meanings are understood clearly.

★

QUESTION: In the sentence *Please have each of the area supervisors file his or her report as soon as he or she reaches the required plateau,* I find the *his/her* and *he/she* combinations annoying. What happened to the old idea of using only masculine forms in such situations?

DR. GRAMMAR: In the last fifteen years or so, many people have come to feel that the use of *he* or *him* to refer to both men and women is sexist. I agree. As a teacher, I would not address a class of men and women by saying, "I want each of you to turn in his homework."

The English language changes to meet social and political needs. Numerous suggestions have been made for this particular problem. One, for instance, is to use *s/he* to replace both *she* and *he* in our vocabulary. So far, none of the proposed changes has excited much attention from the broad base of users. I suspect that at some time in the future this part of our language will indeed change. Until then, you should use the double reference to both sexes.

In many instances, of course, you can easily resolve the problem by making your subject plural.

☞ A doctor must maintain good rapport with *his or her* patients.

☞ Doctors must maintain good rapport with *their* patients.

☞ A great teacher is an inspiration to *his/her* students.

☞ Good teachers are an inspiration to *their* students.

It should be obvious that in those instances when you know the gender of the person mentioned, use it. If your doctor is a woman, use female pronouns.

☞ My doctor asked me to see *her* again next week.

If your lawyer is a man, use male pronouns.

☞ I called my lawyer and told *him* about the changes I want made in my will.

★

QUESTION: Is there a difference between the two sentences *She spoke all morning* and *She has spoken all morning*?

DR. GRAMMAR: Yes. It rests with the difference in the verb tenses.

The first sentence uses the *simple past* tense. This tense indicates that an action began and was completed in the past.

The second sentence uses the *present perfect* tense. Its function is to indicate that an action started in the past and is still going on or was recently completed. The speaker in the second example may, in fact, still be speaking. One can't tell from the sentence.

Another function of the present perfect tense is to indicate repeated action in the past. Look at the difference between the following sentence pairs. The first sentence in each set is in the simple past tense and describes a one-time completed action; the second sentence is in the present perfect tense and describes an action that is repeated.

☞ I *visited* my sister in Boston last Christmas.

☞ I *have visited* my sister in Boston many times.

☞ Gene *spoke* to the board about his needs.

☞ Gene *has spoken* to the board several times about his needs.

★

QUESTION: I can never remember when to use *will* and when to use *shall.* What is the rule?

DR. GRAMMAR: Please let Dr. Grammar put your mind to rest. Years ago, grammarians made a major distinction between these two words (I allude to this in my introduction, page xix). Accepted usage is constantly evolving and changing, and today we have discarded that distinction. Use whichever of the words you are most comfortable with in any given situation.

★

QUESTION: I always thought the word was *burnt,* as in *burnt* toast. Now I find out there is no such word, that it is *burned* toast.

DR. GRAMMAR: It *is* burned toast. *Burnt* is an older form now seldom used. Your original problem was one of pronunciation, not grammar. It is easy for us to hear an *-ed* ending as a *t.* When we write it, we naturally write what we think we have heard. The grammar principle involved is that the verb form used as an adjective is always the participle form of the verb. Maybe these sentences will help:

☞ A car that *has been wrecked* becomes a *wrecked* car.
☞ Money that *has been stolen* is known as *stolen* money.
☞ A person who *has retired* from a job is a *retired* person.

★

QUESTION: Is the subjunctive verb form still used? If so, when?

DR. GRAMMAR: Although some uses of the subjunctive are considered archaic, certain other uses are retained by those who have a keen ear for the language. Here are the three principal uses of what is known as the *subjunctive* that remain in our language:

1. The subjunctive in *if* and *though* clauses: If you have an *if* or *though* clause that expresses a condition contrary to fact, or that is highly improbable or doubtful, select your verb(s) carefully. Use *past tense* verb forms to express *present tense;* use *past perfect tense* verb forms to express *past tense.*

☞ If my grandfather *were* still alive [he isn't], he could answer your question.

☞ He acts as though he *were* the only person in the room, but he isn't.

☞ If I *had been* there with you, I would have helped.

When the *if* or *though* clause states a condition that is possible or likely, the verb form fits the normal tense pattern.

☞ If I *live* through this [I probably will], I'll never criticize anyone again.

☞ If Mr. Kane *was* on campus last Wednesday [he may well have been], I did not see him.

2. The subjunctive in clauses that show a necessity or a demand: If your sentence expresses a necessity, a demand, or even an especially strong request, you need to use the subjunctive form of the verb in the clause that follows it.

☞ I demand that I *be permitted* to speak to the entire committee.

THE SUBJUNCTIVE

50

☞ It is mandatory that you *be* here thirty minutes before your shift begins.

☞ He strongly recommended that Dave *be* more attentive to his work assignment.

In those instances when the verb is other than *to be,* use the regular present tense for all three persons, but you should not add an *s* to the third-person singular.

☞ I request that the desk *remain* exactly where I have positioned it.

☞ Ms. Leveridge will require that the secretary *retype* the report to correct these errors.

☞ I ask that Dave *work* directly with Felicia on all future assignments.

3. The subjunctive in *wish* clauses: When your sentence begins with *I wish, you wish, she wishes, they wish,* use a subjunctive form of the verb in the clause that immediately follows. For present time in the dependent clause, use a verb in the past tense. If the verb is a form of *to be,* use *were* for all three persons.

☞ I wish I *were* there with you today for your graduation.

☞ Imani wishes she *were* that creative.

For past time in the dependent clause, use the past perfect tense.

☞ I wish I *had been* there for your graduation yesterday.

☞ Imani wishes she *had been* more creative in her high-school art classes.

★

QUESTION: What is the difference between the active and the passive voice in writing? Isn't one usually considered better than the other?

DR. GRAMMAR: In the construction known in grammar as the active voice, the subject of the sentence performs the action of the verb, usually on a specific object.

☞ Derek hit the ball.
☞ Ms. Schwartz fired Gloria today.

Both sentences are in the active voice. Derek did the hitting (the acting, if you will) and the ball received the action. Ms. Schwartz did the firing (the acting, again), and Gloria was the object of that action.

In the passive voice, the action passes back to the subject.

☞ The ball was hit by Derek.
☞ Gloria was fired today by Ms. Schwartz.

In these last two examples, the action passes backward from the verb to the subject rather than forward to the object. You can see, too, that even in the short examples the passive-voice sentences are longer. Use of the passive voice tends to weaken writing style.

The single most important part of speech in an English sentence is the verb. You must select your verbs carefully if you are to make your writing have impact. Do not weaken your sentences by using the passive voice unnecessarily.

The passive voice always uses some form of the verb *to be: is, are, was, were, be, being, been.* They are the ones that most readily come to mind when you are writing in a hurry. But they are not necessarily the best. Stop and think about your verb choices. And do not overuse the passive voice.

SECTION TWO:

IN WHICH DR. GRAMMAR

ANSWERS QUESTIONS

ABOUT USAGE

Good words are worth much, and cost little.

—George Herbert, *Jacular Prudentum*

QUESTION: I often become confused with words that sound alike but are spelled differently and have different meanings. For example, I don't always know when to use *whose* and *who's* or *to* and *too*.

DR. GRAMMAR: What concerns you here is usage, the way we use certain parts of our language in certain situations. It has been agreed, for instance, that some words (*advice* and *effect,* for instance) are nouns and that other words (*advise* and *affect*) are verbs. Knowing which word to use in which situation is a difficulty most of us have. The best solution is to commit to memory the function of the words you use most often and to consult your dictionary to check the function of those about which you are unsure.

Here are some of the words that Dr. Grammar is most often asked about and the way I suggest they be used. Notice that they all have a common characteristic: the apostrophe in the shortened or contracted form, no apostrophe in the possessive form.

Its, It's

Its is a possessive pronoun. This word is always used to show ownership.

☞ The bird flew back to *its* nest.
☞ The rare vase fell off *its* pedestal.

It's is the contracted or shortened form of *it is*. Use this form when you need both the subject *it* and the verb *is* in your sentence.

☞ *It's* getting too late in the year for us to think about vacation plans.
☞ If you leave the dent in your car door, *it's* going to rust and make a hole.

Now look at these sentences that use both forms correctly:

☞ The fern is losing *its* leaves because *it's* getting too much water.
☞ *It's* not in the best interest of the committee to flex *its* authority in this matter.

When in doubt about which to use, ask yourself if "it is" can be substituted into the sentence; if it can, use *it's,* if it can't, use *its.*

Whose, Who's

The same usage problem is present with *whose* and *who's*. *Whose* is a possessive pronoun that is used to show ownership.

☞ Christiana is the tour guide *whose* promotion was so highly deserved. [The promotion is Christiana's; it belongs to her.]

☞ *Whose* books are spread all over the kitchen table? [Who owns or possesses the books?]

Who's is the contracted or shortened form of *who is*. Use this form only when you need both the subject *who* and the verb *is*.

☞ *Who's* handling the mail while Linda is on vacation?

☞ Do you know *who's* going to introduce the speaker at the meeting?

☞ I like a person *who's* reliable.

Their, They're, There

The same clues that help to distinguish *its/it's* and *whose/who's* should also guide you in the correct usage of *their, they're,* and *there*. Remember: There is no apostrophe in the possessive pronoun, but the contraction has one.

Their is a possessive pronoun that is always used to show ownership and always refers to a plural noun.

☞ The students took *their* test last Wednesday. [Whose test? The students' test.]

☞ The employees rushed to the pay window to get *their* checks. [Whose checks? The employees' checks.]

They're is the shortened or contracted form of *they are*. Use it only when you need the subject *they* and the verb *are*.

☞ *They're* going to test the new gas lines next Friday afternoon.

☞ The coordinators have announced that *they're* conducting orientation sessions next Monday.

There is used for direction or location.

☞ Put your extra tools *there* beside the workbench.

☞ Please sit over *there*.

There is also used as an expletive. [An *expletive* is a word used to fill out a sentence, often to start one.]

☞ *There* are at least 200 people here.

☞ *There* might be just cause for her resignation.

Your, You're

Your is a possessive pronoun and should always be used when you want to show ownership.

☞ Give the job *your* best effort.

☞ Is this *your* jacket?

You're is the shortened or contracted form of *you are* and should be used only when you need both the subject *you* and the verb *are*.

☞ I hope that *you're* going to be at the meeting tomorrow morning.

☞ *You're* simply going to have to arrange your schedule so it will be flexible.

To, Too, Two

These three words cause some usage confusion, but any problems usually come about when you are writing too fast and do not stop to think clearly enough about which word you need to use. *To* is a preposition that is always used to show a sense of direction, movement, or location.

☞ Take your money *to* the bank.

☞ Call me when you get *to* the office.

Too is used for something that is *excessive*.

☞ This candy is *too* sweet.

☞ Sometimes I think you are just *too* kind.

Two is the easy one in this set because it is always used as a number:

☞ I made *two* calls at home last night.

☞ Place the *two* reports on my desk.

Cite, Site, Sight

Cite is a verb that means to quote or to mention.

☞ Marion *cited* several local authorities in her report on water pollution in the suburbs.

☞ Don't forget to *cite* all your references in the bibliography of your term paper.

Site is a noun that means a place.

☞ The *site* of the new warehouse will be in Lake County.

☞ Chicago was to have been the *site* of the next World's Fair, but the logistics could not be worked out.

Sight is also a noun. It means the ability to see, either physically or mentally.

☞ The operation miraculously restored her *sight*.

☞ Don't lose *sight* of the fact that Crammer was never qualified for the job in the first place.

☞ The *site* of the new golf course is a *sight* to behold.

As a noun, *sight* can also be used like this:

☞ He aimed at the target through the telescopic *sight*.

Sight can also be a verb:

☞ Columbus *sighted* land on October 12, 1492.

CITE, SITE, OR SIGHT?

The similar-sounding sets of words on the last several pages are the ones that seem to bother people the most. At least 80 percent of Dr. Grammar's calls concern the proper usage of those words. But there are indeed others. Here are some other "problem pairs," their order of presentation reflecting the frequency of queries to my grammar hot line.

Passed, Past

Passed is a verb form. Notice the *-ed* ending. It is the typical simple past ending of many verbs and designates a completed action at some earlier time.

☞ I *passed* the algebra test with no difficulty.
☞ We *passed* your house on our way to the park.

Past means in a time gone by, not in the present. It can also mean beyond, as in direction or time.

☞ The era when the New York Yankees won all their baseball games is long *past* now.
☞ It was *past* the child's bedtime.
☞ You can find vending machines in the hallway just *past* the public telephones.

Course, Coarse

A *course* is a plan or a path.

☞ I am taking a *course* in business law.
☞ They are building a lovely bicycle *course* around parts of the lake.

Something that is *coarse* is rough, of low quality, or crude.

☞ He removed the old varnish with elbow grease and *coarse* sandpaper.

☞ Those old green army blankets were *coarse* and scratchy.

☞ Mr. Holmes's *coarse* language and off-color jokes embarrassed everyone.

Plain, Plane

If something is *plain,* it is simple or clear.

☞ Say it in *plain* English, please!

☞ The concept was made quite *plain* to everyone in the class.

But *plain* can also mean not physically attractive, unadorned, or a stretch of relatively level land.

☞ The girl's face was *plain,* but her bright eyes were alive with mischief.

☞ She wore a *plain* blue coat and no hat.

☞ The rain in Spain stays mainly in the *plain.* (Many thanks to Lerner and Loewe!)

A *plane* is, of course, an aircraft, but it can also be a carpenter's tool or even a level of development or accomplishment.

☞ The first time I ever flew on a *plane* was on a Boeing 727.

☞ I needed a *plane* to smooth the door so it would close properly.

☞ It is high time we moved this conversation to a higher *plane* of thinking.

Peace, Piece

Peace means contentment or calm, being free from stress and strife.

☞ We all need to find a private place for some *peace* and quiet these days.

☞ World *peace* is worth striving for.

Piece means a portion or a part, a specimen, or a work of literature or music.

☞ I think there is one more *piece* of pie left on the kitchen table.

☞ We have requested five new *pieces* of furniture for the lobby of our building.

☞ The piano concert included three short *pieces* by Schumann.

Weather, Whether

Weather refers to atmospheric conditions.

☞ We are planning to go the beach Saturday if the *weather* is good.

☞ The *weather* outside is frightful, but, as the song goes, the fire is so delightful.

Whether is used to suggest possibility; it can frequently be exchanged with *if.*

☞ Please ask Frances *whether* she intends to go to the concert Friday night.

☞ Please ask Frances *if* she intends to go to the concert Friday night.

☞ *Whether* she can travel by air is up to her physician.

☞ It's up to her physician *if* she can travel by air.

☞ Please ask the receptionist *whether* the office is open on Saturday during the summer months.

☞ Please ask the receptionist *if* the office is open on Saturday during the summer months.

Whether can also introduce alternatives:

☞ *Whether* you go to Los Angeles or to San Francisco, you'll have a wonderful vacation.

Principal, Principle

Principal is usually used to mean major or most important. It can also be used to refer to the amount of money borrowed on a loan.

☞ Dr. Gorman is the new *principal* of Polk Park High School.

☞ The Love and Temko families are the *principal* developers of the riverfront project.

☞ The speaker presented his *principal* idea in the first five minutes, then bored us for the next twenty-five.

☞ Your monthly mortgage payment of $2020.45 includes both the *principal* and the interest.

Principle is a code, a law, or a rule of behavior or operation.

☞ This country was established on the *principle* of freedom and justice for all.

☞ He had no *principles*; he cheated everyone.

☞ If you understand the operational *principle* behind our organization, you will come to understand the chain of command and its importance to our success.

Here is the use of *principal* and *principle* in one sentence:

☞ If you have trouble deciding if the person in charge of the school is a *principle* or a *principal,* here's a good old principle to follow: A princi*pal* is your friend.

Compliment, Complement

Compliment can be used either as a noun or a verb, but it always means to praise. One good way to remember its definition correctly is to remember that *compliment,* like *praise,* has an *i* tucked right in the middle.

☞ I want to *praise* you on your fine presentation.

☞ I want to *compliment* you on your fine presentation.

☞ The *praise* you received was something you rightly deserved.

☞ The *compliment* you received was something you rightly deserved.

Complement means to complete or the quantity or number needed to make a thing complete. You can remember its usage if you remember that, like *complete,* it has an *e* near its middle.

☞ The Oriental rugs *complement* the office decor nicely.

☞ The red wine was a perfect *complement* to the roast beef.

☞ There was a full *complement* of soldiers stationed at the border.

Already, All Ready

Already means previously, in the past.

☞ Susan had *already* left for the mountains when I received the call.

☞ I have *already* cautioned you once about your excessive absences at work.

All ready means prepared. Note, too, that *all ready* is always written as two separate words. There is no such word in the English language as *allready.*

☞ The students were *all ready* to leave on the field trip when the bus arrived.

☞ The alderman's report was *all ready* to be mailed.

Altogether, All Together

Altogether means entirely or totally. It should be used only in those cases where you could use *entirely* or *totally* in its place and not alter the meaning of your sentence.

☞ The report is *altogether* too long to submit to the committee. [The report is *entirely* too long to submit to the committee.]

☞ Those of us who worked at the front desk were *altogether* opposed to the new work schedule. [Those of us who worked at the front desk were *totally* opposed to the new work schedule.]

All together means all in a group. Notice that it is two separate words, not "alltogether."

☞ The reports from the various supervisors are *all together* on the table. [There are several separate reports gathered into a single whole.]

☞ The students were *all together* in their opposition to the tuition hike. [The entire student body was united in their opposition to the tuition hike.]

Awhile, A while

The difference between *awhile* (one word) and *a while* (two words) depends upon how they are used in a given sentence. *Awhile* is always used as an adverb.

☞ He rested *awhile*. [That is, he rested for a short period of time.]

A while (two words) are an article and a noun.

☞ I need *a while* to think about the problem before I can give you a decision.

☞ Stay for *a while* and let me get you some coffee.

A while is always used after for.

☞ Rest *awhile*.
☞ Rest here for *a while*.

Beside, Besides

Use *beside* if you mean next to or along side of.

☞ I want to sit *beside* the company's owner at the dinner party.
☞ Put the vase of flowers *beside* the lamp on the dresser.

Use *besides* if you mean in addition to.

☞ I am too tired to go to the meeting tonight; *besides,* I have no real interest in the topic. [In addition to the fact that I am tired, I have no interest in the topic.]
☞ *Besides* Joan and me, the Allens sat at the dais at the company dinner.

Everyday, Every Day

Everyday (one word) is an adjective that means commonplace, ordinary, occurring daily.

☞ Gathering around the photocopier for the latest gossip is not an *everyday* occurrence around this office.
☞ I sometimes find myself humming the words to that

old song "These Are the Dreams of the *Everyday* Housewife."

Every day (two words) is used when you want to describe something that takes place as a separate action each day.

☞ I've been getting up at 5:30 A.M. *every day* for the last six months.

☞ We all appreciate the work Martha has done for us at our switchboard *every day* for the last twenty-four weeks.

Can, May

Can is used when you want to suggest ability.

☞ I know that Lauren *can* do the job if she tries. [Lauren has the ability to do the job.]

☞ *Can* you finish the design work and print our brochures by tomorrow morning? [Do you have the ability to finish the design work and print the brochures?]

May is used when you want to suggest permission or possibility.

☞ Gerald *may* go to lunch if he can find someone to take his calls. [He has permission to go to lunch.]

☞ I think Gerald *may* be going to the movies later this evening. [There is the possibility of his going.]

Accept, Except

If you *accept* something or someone, you take or receive that thing or person.

> ☞ During these last few months, I have come to *accept* you as a unique person.
>
> ☞ Please *accept* our best wishes for success in your new endeavor.

If you *except* something or someone, you exclude that thing or person. *Except* is often interchangeable with *but*.

> ☞ Everyone *except* Foley finished the job on time.
>
> ☞ Everyone finished the examination *except* me.
>
> ☞ Dorothy *excepted* herself from the panel because she felt she might be prejudiced.

Adapt, Adopt

Adapt means to adjust or to change in order to make suitable.

> ☞ Carl must *adapt* to the new policies if he is going to last at the job. [Carl must change to make himself suitable to the job.]
>
> ☞ Animals in the wild must *adapt* to severe changes in their environment or die.
>
> ☞ When I got my first job, I tried to *adapt* what I had learned in psychology classes so that I could work successfully with two dozen strangers. [I tried to make applicable what I had learned in psychology to fit a particular situation.]

Adopt means to take charge of or to put into effect in the same form.

☞ Brian and Susan waited two years before they were able to *adopt* an infant. [They brought the child into their home and took charge of him or her.]

☞ When I became an administrator, I'm afraid I *adopted* the policies of my old business-law teacher, Dr. Wright. [I took Dr. Wright's policies and tried to make them work for me.]

Advice, Advise

Advice is a noun meaning counsel.

☞ I gave him some fatherly *advice* about his work habits.

☞ Helen asked me for *advice* about the new contract.

Advise is a verb meaning to give counsel.

☞ After seeing the report, I *advised* him that I thought it should be redone.

☞ I *advised* Helen about company policy on processing new contracts.

Affect, Effect

Affect is a verb, and it means to change or to influence.

☞ Changing the working hours *affected* the morale of the entire shift.

☞ The low circulation of the new magazine *affected* the board's decision to discontinue its publication at the end of the year.

Effect as a noun describes the result or end product of something that has taken place or that always exists.

☞ The background music at work has a very positive *effect* on my performance.

☞ The *effect* of the moonlight on the lake was wonderfully romantic.

Effect as a verb means to cause something to happen.

☞ Her resignation *effected* several changes in procedures for the shipping department.

☞ You really need to *effect* a change in the attitude you display to your fellow workers.

★

QUESTION: Does it matter if I use *continuous* or *continual* interchangeably? Can I say "My baby cried continuously all night long"?

DR. GRAMMAR: Well, if your baby cried *continuously* throughout an entire night, he or she must have lungs worthy of an entry in the *Guinness Book of World Records*. *Continuous* means without stopping, with absolutely no breaks. To be accurate, I hope you meant to say, "My baby cried *continually* all night long."

Continual is used to describe an action that happens at intervals, something that happens repeatedly over a period of time. It is not something that goes on nonstop.

☞ They held a *continuous* vigil at the county court-house.

☞ My teenager talked on the telephone *continuously* for eight hours. [This might indeed be true, but Dr. Grammar suspects that even the teenager in question talked *continually,* not *continuously*!]

☞ The *continual* clanking of the trolley kept us awake all night.

☞ After we had won the state high-school spelling contest, my telephone rang *continually* with congratulations.

Raised thus far in this chapter have been what are called "problem pairs" or "confused sets" of words. There are many other pairs or sets of words that I do not consider so much "confused" as "misused." Most of us recognize that there are indeed differences in the words just presented and that those differences are often quite basic to English grammar. There is, for instance, a grammatical difference between *whose* and *who's* and between *there* and *they're*.

But with the "misused" pairs there is no such distinction. One may not even be aware that there is a distinction at all. Conscientious writers and speakers try to be aware of the distinctions, however subtle, when they communicate, because they are striving to be accurate in their writing and speech.

Here are some of the "misused" pairs that Dr. Grammar has had to clarify repeatedly for users:

Appraise, Apprise

Appraise means to judge or evaluate.

☞ Have someone *appraise* your ring so you can insure it.

☞ The *appraisal* on the property was too low to secure the loan.

Apprise means to inform.

☞ Please *apprise* Mr. Jensen of his constitutional rights.

☞ The brochure from the personnel office is designed to *apprise* you of all the insurance benefits for which you are qualified.

Comprise, Compose

Comprise means to contain or to include.

☞ Canada *comprises* ten provinces, the Yukon, and the Northwest Territories.

☞ This report *comprises* the best thinking of the ten members of this committee in the last six months.

Compose means to make up or to constitute.

☞ I need to *compose* my thoughts so I can write a coherent report.

☞ Canada is *composed* of ten provinces, the Yukon, and the Northwest Territories.

Remember that the whole *comprises* the parts. The parts *compose* the whole.

Conscious, Conscience

Conscious means having an awareness of one's thoughts and/or existence.

☞ He wasn't *even conscious* that he had offended anyone by his horrible behavior.

☞ His remarks were a *conscious* insult to Steve.

☞ She was certainly *conscious* of the fact that it was her turn to work the night shift.

Of course, it also means being awake or aware, as:

☞ We ran over to the fallen child, trying to see if he were *conscious*.

Conscience is the sense of recognizing between right and wrong with regard to one's actions.

☞ A clear *conscience* brings peace of mind.

☞ I just don't know how his *conscience* will let him sleep after all he has done to harm me and my family.

Sensual, Sensuous

Sensual is used to describe physical or sexual feelings.

☞ Even the perfume ads in magazines these days depend upon *sensual* pictures to sell their products.

☞ The German director Fassbinder often depicted *sensual* scenes in his films.

Sensuous is used to describe a feeling of the senses but is not necessarily tied to anything sexual. It is used to indicate an awareness of feelings.

> ☞ An early spring day can provide a *sensuous* experience for almost everyone.
> ☞ The mellow jazz, the soft lights, and the muted colors in the room created a lush, *sensuous* atmosphere.

Explicit, Implicit

Explicit means plainly or clearly stated.

> ☞ Greg's comments about the concert were quite *explicit.*
> ☞ I gave you *explicit* instructions, and for some reason you elected to ignore them.

Implicit means understood but not stated.

> ☞ We had an *implicit* understanding about what we expected of each other.
> ☞ She did not need to say anything; her feelings were quite *implicit* by day's end.

Infer, Imply

Infer means to arrive at a conclusion, to draw an unstated opinion.

> ☞ From his remarks, I *inferred* that he was interested in the position.

☞ Considering the high price, you correctly *inferred* that the car would still be for sale.

Imply means to suggest, perhaps indirectly.

☞ His remarks seemed to *imply* that he was interested in the position.
☞ I merely *implied* that I might be interested.

Remember that a speaker always *implies* and a listener always *infers*.

Few, Less

Few is used with items that can be counted, with what grammar texts call "count nouns."

☞ Susan has a *few* questions to ask at the meeting.
☞ There were *fewer* people at the conference this year than there were last year.
☞ It seems to me that there are *fewer* coats on sale than usual.

In each instance above, *few* or *fewer* comes immediately in front of a noun that can be counted. You could count the number of questions, the number of people, the number of coats.

Less is used with nouns that cannot be counted, which are called "mass nouns," and to express amounts and degrees.

☞ Put *less* air in the tire.
☞ We eat *less* cheese than we used to.

☞ Our company has *less* overhead than our competitors.

☞ It takes far *less* effort today to do housework than it did a century ago.

In these examples, *less* comes in front of the mass nouns. You can't count concepts such as overhead or effort, and the amounts of air and cheese are not ordinarily quantifiable as distinct units.

Like, As

Like and *as* are used in comparisons. The trick is to know when to use which. In grammatical jargon, *like* is a preposition and is used with nouns and pronouns. *As* is a conjunction and is used with clauses that contain verbs.

☞ George acted *like* an idiot at the office party.

☞ It's just *like* old times with Doris back at the reception desk.

☞ During the program review, please carry on *as* you ordinarily would.

☞ Don't do *as* I do; do *as* I tell you. [With apologies to the old saying.]

Anxious, Eager

Anxious means looking forward to something with apprehension or dread, or being very worried. Remember, the word is a relative of anxiety.

☞ Eugene was quite *anxious* about the job interview. [Eugene was apprehensive about the interview.]

☞ I *anxiously* await the final exam next week. [I dread the final exam next week.]

Eager means looking forward to something with desire, not dread.

☞ I am *eager* to hear about your summer plans. [I really want to hear about them.]

☞ I was very *anxious* about meeting my new supervisor, but she seemed *eager* to join our department. [I was apprehensive about meeting her, but she was looking forward to her new job.]

Jealousy, Envy

Jealousy means heightened suspicion, resentment, protection.

☞ Harry has always been a *jealous* spouse. [Harry has always been a suspicious husband.]

☞ Martha keeps a *jealous* guard over her jewelry when she travels. [Martha protects her jewelry carefully.]

Envy suggests an unnatural desire for another's possessions or good fortune.

☞ Jane was *envious* of Martha's jewelry. [Jane wished she, rather than Martha, owned the jewelry.]

☞ Keith *envied* Sarah her new position at the bank. [Keith wished he, rather than Sarah, had the job at the bank.]

☞ Robert was *envious* of his best friend's good luck in Las Vegas. [Robert wished he had won as much money as his friend.]

☞ I *envy* your lovely teeth. [I wish I had teeth like yours.]

Farther, Further

Farther suggests physical distance. Remember that it begins with *far,* a word marking distance.

☞ My new house is *farther* away from where I work, but it's a much nicer neighborhood.

☞ The second playroom is *farther* along the hallway.

In both of these examples, you could physically measure the distance in feet or miles.

Further suggests figurative distance, usually a distance of time, degree, or space.

☞ Frank is sinking *further* and *further* into debt.

☞ The construction work is *further* along than we had expected it to be by this time of the year.

☞ Alexandra has gone much *further* with her career plans than anyone anticipated.

Amount, Number

Amount is used for "mass nouns"—ideas or things that can't be counted individually. *Number* is used for "count nouns"—individual items that can be counted.

☞ Ten million dollars is a large *amount* of money for anyone to inherit.

☞ There is a small *amount* of coffee left in the pot.

☞ The *amount* of time I have spent on the Fipps project far exceeds its worth.

In each of these examples, we are discussing mass nouns: money, coffee, and time.

☞ The *number* of calls quickly tripled after the story in the *Trib* came out.

☞ Can you guess the *number* of jellybeans in the jar?

☞ The *number* of hours I spent on the Fipps project far exceeds its worth.

In the three examples above, we are discussing telephone calls, jellybeans, and hours, all items that can be counted.

Bring, Take

Bring indicates movement toward the speaker.

☞ *Bring* the report to me.

☞ Sharon *brought* the books to our committee meeting.

Take indicates movement away from the speaker.

☞ Be certain to *take* your umbrella, in case it rains.

☞ Remember to *take* your lunch tomorrow, because the cafeteria will be closed.

In each of the examples, the speaker is not going with the person to whom he or she is making the suggestion.

☞ *Bring* the documents with you tomorrow so that I may *take* them to the board.

☞ Would you *bring* an extra umbrella for me; I left mine on the train.

☞ Please *bring* an extra copy of the report for Ms. McKay.

In each of the three examples above, the speaker is in the same place as the person to whom he or she is speaking. A little rule helps: bring *to;* take *from.*

Percent, Percentage

Percent is used with a number.

☞ Fifty *percent* of the orders were lost.

☞ Take an additional 25 *percent* off the list price.

Percentage is used without the number reference. It indicates a general size.

☞ A small *percentage* of their sales will be affected by the merger.

☞ We are not concerned about the 30 *percent* drop in profits, only about the *percentage* of customers we lost.

★

QUESTION: Is it correct English to say, "I graduated from high school"?

DR. GRAMMAR: Although many people use this construction, the more formal usage is, "I was graduated from high school." Technically speaking, you did not graduate, the school graduated you; you were graduated. Whichever you choose, avoid at all costs the deplorable "I graduated high school."

★

QUESTION: I read in our local newspaper that Jane Bullock *was wed* to Todd Hammerfest. And in another column in the same paper I read that Mr. Garrison *wedded* Ms. Ricards. Are both verb forms correct? Is this all simply a part of journalistic style?

DR. GRAMMAR: An old sexist rule, not of grammar but of etiquette and tradition, says that *a man weds a woman* but *the woman is wedded* or *married to the man.* If you wish to give any of this an aura of pseudo-grammatical respectability, you might say that the verb *to wed* and its various synonyms take the passive voice when the subject is feminine and the active voice when the subject is masculine: He *marries* her; she *is married to* him.

   This is one of many instances where Dr. Grammar feels that the artificial and, in this case especially, sexist guidelines in our language go too far. I think we can agree that the man marries the woman and the woman marries the man. There!

★

QUESTION: A secretary in my office made a major fuss the other day when I dictated *on behalf of* and she argued that it should have been *in behalf of.* Is there really a difference?

DR. GRAMMAR: Yes, there is a difference, however subtle it may be. *On behalf* means acting in another's place. *In behalf* means acting in another's interest.

☞ Mr. Jenkins could not be here this morning, so Ms. Lerner is acting *on his behalf.* [She is taking his place.]

☞ *On behalf* of the president, I welcome you to Oakton Community College. [I am acting in the president's place.]

☞ The lawyer spoke forcefully *in behalf* of her client. [The lawyer spoke for her client's interest.]

☞ Renée was acting *in behalf* of her mother's estate. [Renée was acting in the interest of her mother's estate.]

★

QUESTION: One of the women I work with always talks about her *future plans.* Isn't that a bit redundant?

DR. GRAMMAR: Yes, yes, yes, if Dr. Grammar may himself be redundant. Do not repeat an idea unnecessarily, even with different words. The idea of a future is contained in the word *plans.* One does not make *plans* for the past.

Alas, it is all too easy for us to lapse into redundancies, because they are around us all the time, especially in the popular media. Look at these typical examples:

✗ The *end result* of the testing is that we will have better drinking water in the village. [The result will of course come at the end. Can you have a beginning result?]

x The president said that he would submit his *final conclusion* by the end of next week. [At whatever point it is reached, a conclusion is final.]

x Let's all *team up together* and join in the fight against child abuse. [How do you team apart?]

x Once you have *mixed together* all of the ingredients, let the dough rise for an hour before shaping it into loaves. [How do you mix something apart?]

x It is my *personal opinion* that we are spending far too much money on national defense and not enough on health care at home. [Your opinion is personal.]

x As soon as I learned of the *serious crisis,* I called the Red Cross to see if there was anything I could do. [A crisis by its very nature is serious.]

x Police reported that they found the *dead body* at the end of a dark alley. [If the body isn't dead, the police found the victim.]

x If we *bond together* on these issues, no one can defeat us. [Try bonding separately.]

x Unfortunately, the speaker got completely off the *subject matter* he was supposed to be discussing. [Unless you are dealing with ghosts, subjects have matter.]

x *At this point in time* there is little we can do but sit and wait. [Just say *now.*]

x In the future, we hope to *advance forward* with the second phase of development. [There is a movie titled *Back to the Future,* but advancing means going forward.]

x With six boxtops, you get a *free gift.* [I didn't know you could pay for a gift.]

REPETITIOUS REDUNDANCIES

In writing, it is wise to remember not to use two words when one will convey the same meaning.

★

QUESTION: My supervisor always uses *impact* as a verb, as in "The Visconti merger will impact heavily on our sales for the next three years at least." Can *impact* be used as a verb?

DR. GRAMMAR: Alas, I have heard that usage all too often. I suspect I am fighting a losing battle when I decry it, but I am still charging valiantly with the old grammatical flag. Let me say that careful writers wouldn't even think of writing or uttering such a sentence. *Impact* is a noun and should be used *only* as a noun.

☞ The Visconti merger will have an *impact* on our sales for the next three years at least.

You might be saying that Dr. Grammar is violating his own rule, using two words when one will do: *impact* is one word; *have an impact* is three. I say, violate any rule rather than say something barbarous.

SECTION THREE:

IN WHICH DR. GRAMMAR

ANSWERS QUESTIONS

ABOUT MECHANICS

There is no room in this country
for hyphenated Americanism. . . .

—Theodore Roosevelt

Marks of punctuation such as the comma, the semicolon, the colon, the period, and even the parentheses are used to guide your reader through your sentences. They serve as markers to help the reader know where the structure of the sentence is going next and to see the proper relationship among the various parts of the sentence. These marks of punctuation work with the grammar of the sentence and are important to both you and your reader in assuring that the reader gains from the sentence the understanding of its meaning that you intended.

Other marks of punctuation—capitalization, italics, hyphens, etc.—have nothing at all to do with the structure of the sentence and its parts. They are more accurately a part of what is sometimes called "the print code." These marks, a part of the mechanics of writing, are simply conventions of writing that have been agreed upon by most writers for a long time. The grammar of a sentence is not incorrect if you fail, for instance, to mark the title of a book with italics or underlining; but you help your reader along if you do, because he or she has come to expect that book titles are italicized or underlined.

★

QUESTION: In school, we were taught to underline the titles of books, plays, and movies and to place quotation marks around the titles of poems and short stories. However, I see in the *Chicago Tribune* that book and movie titles are also placed within quotation marks. Were we taught wrong fifteen years ago, or have the rules changed?

DR. GRAMMAR: You were taught correctly, but what the *Chicago Tribune* uses is a correct journalistic style. For many, many years, journalistic style has differed on some points from other forms of published writing. These differences came from a variety of influences. Foremost among them were the limitations of type design available to many newspapers and the limitations of time to write copy and set type in a newspaper office. Although the computer age has overcome these factors, newspapers continue to follow their traditional style. Newspapers still tend to use quotation marks around the titles of books, movies, plays, operas, television programs, and works of art. Academic and business writing, on the other hand, prefers that those same titles be underlined or printed in italics.

   ☞ Journalism: "Gone With the Wind" (book and movie)
   ☞ Academic and Business: *Gone With the Wind*

☞ Journalism: "Madam Butterfly" (opera)
☞ Academic and Business: *Madama Butterfly* [Journalists usually translate a foreign title into English unless the work is known only by its original title.]

☞ Journalism: "Long Day's Journey into Night" (play)
☞ Academic and Business: *Long Day's Journey into Night*

☞ Journalism: "Cheers," "Designing Women" (television programs)
☞ Academic and Business: *Cheers, Designing Women*

☞ Journalism: Rodin's "The Thinker" (work of art)
☞ Academic and Business: Rodin's *The Thinker*

However, everyone—journalists and academic and business writers—agrees that quotation marks should be used around the titles of poems, short stories, songs, and short musical compositions.

☞ Joyce Kilmer's "Trees" (poem)
☞ Anton Chekhov's "Gooseberries" (short story)
☞ Bob Dylan's "Mr. Tambourine Man" (song)
☞ Heinrich Schmitz's "Cardamom Rhapsody" (short musical composition)
☞ Eric Zorn's "Hometowns" (newspaper column)

★

QUESTION: When I am writing the title of a poem or a book, I never know what words to capitalize, so I just capitalize them all; and I've seen it done this way in print. But I wonder if there is another way.

DR. GRAMMAR: The general standards of the print code say that you should capitalize the initial letter in the first and the last words of all titles, regardless of what they are, and that you should capitalize the initial letter of all other words in the title except the articles, short prepositions, and short conjunctions.

☞ Bacon's essay "On Reading" is still a favorite of mine.

☞ Stanley Kubrick's *2001* is too enigmatic for me.

☞ My son is reading *The Red Badge of Courage* in his sophomore English class.

☞ *Word Processing for the Beginning Student* has been a useful book.

☞ *Test Your Word Power* really does.

Also capitalize articles, short prepositions, and short conjunctions when they are the first word in a subtitle.

☞ We use *Writing for Today: A Practical Rhetoric* in my freshman class.

☞ "Visitation: Or Some Call It Love" is an excellent article that all parents separated from their children should read.

★

QUESTION: How do I write the title that precedes a person's name? I know that *Mr., Mrs.,* and *Ms.* are always written in abbreviated form, but what about professional titles such as *Doctor* and *Professor?*

NAMES WITH TITLES

DR. GRAMMAR: Certain titles of address are always abbreviated when they are used with a proper name: *Mr., Mrs., Ms., Dr.,* and *St.*

Mr. Whipple   Ms. Franz   St. Thomas

Certain other titles—especially *Prof., Capt., Rep.,* and *Sen.*—are abbreviated only when they are used with the full name. If these titles are used with the last name only, they should be spelled out completely.

Prof. George Wilson   Professor Wilson
Sen. Marianne Leads   Senator Leads

★

QUESTION: My physician sends his bill on stationery that reads "Dr. Walter J. Elicot, M.D." My husband thinks this is pretentious and that our physician should use either *Dr.* or *M.D.,* but not both. What do you think?

DR. GRAMMAR: I think your husband is correct. A title that comes before a name should not contain the same information that is indicated in a degree designation following the name. Your doctor should correctly show his name as "Dr. Walter J. Elicot" or "Walter J. Elicot, M.D."

Similarly, a minister who has a doctor of divinity degree may be known as the Reverend Gregory Norris, D.D., or the Reverend Dr. Gregory Norris. But he should not be addressed as the Reverend Dr. Gregory Norris, D.D. That is repeating the degree information.

★

QUESTION: I have had a discussion with my uncle on how to punctuate a sentence that ends with a person's honors and so ends with an abbreviation. I say that I need two periods, one after the title and one for the sentence itself. My uncle says one period is all that is needed. Who is right? Tickets to a Bears' football game rest on this one.

ANSWER: Sorry, but your uncle is going to enjoy the game at your expense. If the sentence ends with any abbreviated term or word that requires a period, do not add another period for the sentence itself. One period is sufficient.

☞ I am going tomorrow to hear the talk on preventative tooth care by Dr. Agnes Silverman, D.D.S.

☞ The thought-provoking discussion about the possibility of life on other planets was led by Edwin Gregg, D.D.

☞ I read the summary of the court case as it was presented by Rudolph P. Nostrom Jr.

☞ Just as soon as possible, I want you to make an appointment with Louise G. Palm, M.D.

★

QUESTION: I was taught to put periods after the individual letters in an abbreviation. For example, I would write I.R.S. for the Internal Revenue Service or A.M.A. for the American Medical Association. But I don't see those periods in print anymore. Is it now permissible simply to write IRS and AMA?

DR. GRAMMAR: In recognized abbreviations of all capital letters, you no longer need to put periods between the letters. Such abbreviations as these are perfectly correct:

| AMA | IRS | NFL |
| MIT | TWA | UN |

As with so much else in the English language, there are exceptions. You do use periods between the letters if the abbreviation is for a geographic name or for an academic degree:

| U. S. S. R. | U. S. A. | U. K. |
| B. A. | M. A. | M. S. |

And certain other common abbreviations still require the period after each letter. The ones most frequently used are A.D., B.C., P.O., and V.P.

★

QUESTION: What is an acronym?

DR. GRAMMAR: An acronym is a shortened reference to a longer form. But unlike the simple abbreviation, the acronym has a system to it. It is composed of the first letter of each of the words that make up the longer form. There are well-known acronyms such as these:

PUSH	People United to Save Humanity
SALT	Strategic Arms Limitation Talks
CORE	Congress of Racial Equality
OPEC	Organization of Petroleum Exporting Countries

What distinguishes an acronym is that it becomes a word in our vocabulary. With abbreviations, you say the letters: You say the three letters of the AMA individually when you refer to the American Medical Association, just as you say all three letters of the FBI when you refer to that government agency. But you do not say the four letters of the acronyms *PUSH* or *OPEC* (pronounced oh-pek); you treat them as words. These are, in fact, words in our vocabulary, words we have coined from longer references. And they can function in sentences in every way that any other word can.

☞ Did you see the news about *OPEC* today?
☞ There will be a new bulletin from *PUSH* headquarters later this afternoon.

Acronyms are written in all capital letters with no periods between the letters.

★

QUESTION: When I write the minutes of our committee meeting, I make notes like, "Two people . . . ." The other person who sometimes takes the minutes always writes, "2 people . . . ." Is there a rule about spelling out numbers?

DR. GRAMMAR: The answer to your immediate question is quite simple. Always spell out the number if it is at the beginning of a sentence, no matter what it is. In your example, you were correct: "Two people . . . ."

Now that I've said that, let me explain that the issue is not all that simple. The general rule is to spell out any numbers that can be written in one or two words and to use figures for the others:

five dollars	2,290 dollars
one assistant	101 assistants

three million workers	3,276 workers
three fourths	1⅝

But even these guidelines get complicated because business writers use a different formula. In most business writing, spell out numbers from one to nine and use figures for all others.

seven invoices	11 invoices
three computers	22 computers
six reports	100 reports

And there are some other special guidelines as well:

Use figures for dates that include the year and the day.

☞ September 1, 1939
☞ July 4, 1776

Use figures for street numbers, but be careful with the name of the street if it is a number.

☞ 1865 Broadway
☞ 1425 East 54th Street
☞ 18 North 36th Place
☞ 2 Innocent Way
☞ 119 West 23rd Street
☞ 47 91st Avenue

The *-th, -st,* or *-rd* suffix may be omitted if an intervening word such as *East* or *North* occurs between the building number and the street.

FIGURES OR WORDS?

☞ 1425 East 54 Street
☞ 18 North 36 Place

If the street name is a number, spell it out if it is *one* through *ten* and use figures for numbers above *ten*.

☞ 343 Third Avenue
☞ 2 Fifth Place
☞ 343 115th Street
☞ 27 42nd Avenue

Finally, do not abbreviate directional signals that precede a street name.

☞ 226 South 56th Street [not S. 56th Street]
☞ 145 North Burton Court [not N. Burton Court]

★

QUESTION: I'm never certain how to show the time of day when I'm writing. Do I always use numbers for the time? Are the designations for morning and evening capitalized?

DR. GRAMMAR: Let me begin with your second question. You can write A.M. and P.M. or a.m. and p.m.; it really doesn't matter at all. This is one of those instances where style manuals let you pick which form to use. Just be consistent and use the same one throughout the same piece of writing. As to your first question, if you use A.M. and P.M. (or a.m. and p.m.) designations, the time reference that precedes them should be in figures (or numbers, if you please).

☞ It is now 9:45 A.M.
☞ It is now 9:45 a.m.

If you do not use the A.M./P.M. designations, you should spell out the time.

☞ Meet me at three tomorrow afternoon.

☞ I'll see you there about one-fifteen.

When you use the word *o'clock*, use figures if your purpose is to stress the time emphatically; otherwise, spell out the word for more formality.

☞ You must meet me at 4 o'clock this afternoon! [This places strong emphasis on a specific time.]

☞ I would like to meet you at four o'clock this afternoon. [Polite and more formal; emphasis is transferred to the meeting, away from the time.]

★

QUESTION: I'm writing a long report for my boss and have to make reference to several chapters and pages in the two books we have been using as sources. Do I spell out the chapter and page numbers, or do I write them as numerals?

DR. GRAMMAR: Chapter and page numbers in a book, magazine, report, and the like are always written as figures.

☞ You will find the reference on *page 5*.

☞ *Chapter 17* is the foundation of our study.

☞ The accounting costs are carefully explained on *page 21* of *chapter 12*.

★

QUESTION: I just got my English paper back from my instructor, and he circled two places where I had used hyphens and told me they were wrong. At the end of one line I used a hyphen to divide *aco-ustics,* and at the end of another line I used a hyphen to divide *learn-ed.* He marked both of these as spelling errors, but they aren't misspelled. What gives?

DR. GRAMMAR: Dr. Grammar would not call these spelling errors, but they *are* departures from the normal print code. That is, you did not write the information according to the usually accepted format.

The most common use of the hyphen is to divide a word that cannot fit on a line of your writing or typing and to carry that word over to the next line. But you must divide a word only between syllables. The first word you mention, *acoustics,* was separated at the wrong point. Check your dictionary and you will see that the syllable break is between the *s* and the *t.* You should have separated the word like this: *acous-tics.* And *learned,* unless you are speaking of a "learned man"—where learned (meaning well-educated or wise) is pronounced as two syllables—should not be divided at all. *Learned* (meaning that knowledge has been acquired) is a one-syllable word.

Some words are tricky, and even a trained ear cannot always tell where the syllable division occurs. It is best to use a dictionary unless you are absolutely sure. Look at these tricky examples:

de-sire	*not*	des-ire
i-vo-ry	*not*	iv-o-ry
sweat-er	*not*	swea-ter

If the word you intend to divide contains a prefix (such as *pre-* or *sub-*) or a suffix (such as *-able* or *-ment*), divide it after the prefix or before the suffix.

sub-standard	*not*	substan-dard
pre-conference	*not*	precon-ference
suit-able	*not*	suita-ble
govern-ment	*not*	gov-ernment

Never hyphenate a word so that a single letter remains at the end of one line or at the beginning of another.

agron-omy	*not*	a-gronomy
neces-sary	*not*	necessar-y
fool-ery	*not*	fooler-y

It is also generally agreed that there is no need to divide a word if you are going to carry only two letters to the next line. After all, the hyphen itself takes up one space where one of the two letters would go; try to squeeze in that one additional letter.

habit	*not*	hab-it
tardy	*not*	tar-dy
lux-ury	*not*	luxu-ry
walked	*not*	walk-ed

It's also good style not to break a proper noun at the end of a line (e.g., Nix-on). And try to avoid double hyphens at the end of a line (e.g., "the middle-man-
agement level . . .").

When you're typing, those are good points of "print code" style to keep in mind.

★

QUESTION: It seems to me that more and more I am seeing two or more words joined by hyphens. Sometimes I like the effect and wish I could use it in my own writing, but I don't understand how it works. Please tell me when I can connect two words with a hyphen.

DR. GRAMMAR: I know what you are asking, and you are right; hyphenated words can add a nice stylistic touch to a piece of writing when used correctly. Use the hyphen to join two or more words to form a single-unit modifier in front of a noun. Look at these examples and see how the hyphenated words are bonded so they function as one modifier and not as two, or in one instance as three, separate modifiers.

☞ That *well-designed* project is nearing completion.
☞ My cousin moved into a *six-story* building.
☞ We use nothing but the *finest-quality* ingredients in our baked goods.
☞ The *four-year-old* child was found wandering around in the cold streets.
☞ Ellen has applied for a *six-month* leave of absence.

When the same two or three words follow the noun, they are not hyphenated.

☞ The project nearing completion is *well designed.*
☞ My cousin moved into a new building *six stories* tall.
☞ Our baked goods are made of ingredients that are nothing but the *finest quality.*
☞ The child who was found wandering around on the cold streets is *four years old.*
☞ Ellen has applied for a leave of absence for *six months.*

The hyphen is not used when an adverb ending in *-ly* is joined with an adjective to form a compound.

☞ The *carefully documented* report was stolen. [Not: The *carefully-documented* report was stolen.]

☞ She always uses the *highly polished* coffee urn. [Not: She always uses the *highly-polished* coffee urn.]

★

QUESTION: I remember someone telling me that the hyphen was good to use to give emphasis to my writing. Is it true that the hyphen can give my writing more emphasis? How?

DR. GRAMMAR: I am not certain that the hyphen can give your writing more emphasis, but sometimes it is needed to give *one word* of your writing more emphasis. Look at the way the hyphen is used in these sentences to help the reader "see" the correct word in the sentence the first time through:

☞ The sculptor *re-formed* the base of the statue. [He formed it again.]

☞ Arthur is a *reformed* alcoholic. [He turned away from his excessive drinking.]

☞ John *re-counted* the day's receipts. [He counted them again.]

☞ Susan *recounted* every detail of her vacation. [She related her trip in endless detail.]

☞ Bring me a stack of *twenty-dollar* bills. [There is a stack of bills, each bill is worth twenty dollars.]

☞ Bring me a stack of *twenty dollar* bills. [There are many dollar bills, and I want a stack of twenty of them.]

Sometimes, the correctly positioned hyphen can help to avoid the possibility of ambiguity in your writing.

☞ Dr. Garrick is in the process of opening a small animal hospital.

Is the hospital to be a small one for animals? Is it for small animals and not large ones? Use of a hyphen would help the reader get the intended meaning.

☞ Dr. Garrick is in the process of opening a small-animal hospital.

Now we know it is a hospital for small animals.

★

QUESTION: Are there special rules for using hyphens when I am writing numbers or when I am using fractions?

DR. GRAMMAR: Use a hyphen when you are writing numbers between twenty-one and ninety-nine.

☞ Allen has *sixty-three* file folders at home.
☞ Ms. Erisman has *twenty-two* phone calls to return this afternoon.

Use a hyphen when you write out fractions used as adjectives, that is, when they are in front of a noun and modify it. If the fraction functions as a noun, do not use a hyphen.

☞ Kelsey reports a *one-fifth* drop in sales. [Here, the fraction acts as an adjective, modifying *drop.*]

☞ Kelsey reports a drop of *one fifth* in sales. [Here, the fraction acts as a noun, in this case an amount.]

☞ We now use *two-thirds* more space than we did during this time last year. [Here, the fraction modifies *space*; it tells how much space.)

☞ *Two thirds* of the space we are now using was not necessary a year ago. [Here, the fraction acts as a noun and does not require a hyphen.]

★

QUESTION: Maybe I'm getting old, but I always put a hyphen between prefixes and their base. But just this morning in the newspaper I read about a *midwife,* not a *mid-wife,* and about *antifreeze,* not *anti-freeze.* Am I wrong in the way I have been writing these words for eons?

DR. GRAMMAR: The English language is slowly but constantly changing, and you are describing one of those processes of change. Let me give you an example to illustrate.

At one time, not terribly long ago, *base ball* was written as two separate words. As base and ball came to be more and more closely associated, they began to appear connected by a hyphen in print: *base-ball.* Eventually, the hyphen disappeared and we had a new word in the English language: *baseball.* The words *football* and *basketball,* incidentally, evolved the same way. In fact, it has been only in the last twenty years that *basketball* has consistently been written as one word.

The trend is to move away from using hyphens with

prefixes and suffixes, except with the prefixes *ex-* and *self-,* and the suffix *-elect.*

☞ ex-president
☞ ex-convict
☞ self-addressed envelope
☞ self-serving interest
☞ mayor-elect
☞ secretary-elect

However, you may use a hyphen to avoid an awkward combination of letters, as in *anti-intellectual* (to avoid the awkward double *i*), and you must use a hyphen when a prefix is used with a word that begins with a capital, as in *anti-Maoist, mid-September,* or *pre-Columbian.*

Dr. Grammar confesses that the guidelines are whimsically followed in many instances. Look at these forms, all considered correct:

co-anchor	coauthor
co-owner	cooperate
co-editor	coeditor
semi-independent	semiopaque

To this day, I always have to pause when I come across "antired" in a sentence.

★

QUESTION: What is the difference between a proper noun and a common noun? I know that one is capitalized and the other is not, but I sometimes have difficulty remembering which is which. Help!

PROPER AND COMMON NOUNS

DR. GRAMMAR: Proper nouns indicate *specific* persons, places, or things. General classes of people, places, or things are called common nouns. Consider the difference in the examples below:

Proper noun: University of Illinois
Common noun: the university

Proper noun: *The Great Gatsby*
Common noun: a novel

Proper noun: Dr. Dooley
Common noun: my doctor

Proper noun: Accounting 328
Common noun: the accounting class

You can readily see that the proper nouns designate a specific university, a specific novel, a specific doctor, even a specific accounting class. The common nouns, on the other hand, refer only to general things (university, novel, doctor, accounting class).

Let me put some nouns in a sentence so you can see that the first italicized word in the sentence is specific (a proper noun that should be capitalized) and that it belongs to the general group labeled by the second italicized word (a common noun that should not be capitalized):

☞ *Chicago* is the largest *city* in the Midwest.
☞ *James* is easily the best *friend* I have ever had.
☞ *Robert Frost* is my favorite *poet.*
☞ *Astor* is the *street* with all those lovely trees.

★

QUESTION: Why aren't the names of the four seasons capitalized anymore? I always used to see them capitalized. Are they now just four more common nouns?

DR. GRAMMAR: The answer to your question points up the ever-changing nature of English. We now have a fairly large set of words that used to be considered proper nouns or adjectives but are used so frequently and are so common in their use that they are considered to be common nouns and are no longer capitalized. They have acquired a generic meaning by becoming commonplace. *Fall, winter, spring,* and *summer* have fallen into this category. They have been used for so long and so often that they are now regarded as commonplace and need not be capitalized, unless they are the first word in the sentence, of course. Look at the following words that are now regarded as common nouns or adjectives, even though they originated from proper nouns:

- ☞ I drink only *pasteurized* milk.
- ☞ Do you prefer *roman* or *arabic* numerals?
- ☞ My aunt has a fabulous collection of bone *china.*
- ☞ He used a plaster of *paris* mold to prepare the shape of the fountain.
- ☞ Although it is quite small, the village is a *mecca* for artists.
- ☞ Mail your response in the *manila* envelope.
- ☞ She always gets a *charley* horse in her right leg after running so far.
- ☞ How many *watts* of electricity does your microwave use?

★

QUESTION: Can you give me some help with the names of my college courses? Do I capitalize them or underline them?

DR. GRAMMAR: You do not underline the names of your college courses, but you do capitalize them if they are the names of specific courses. You might take *history* as a general field of study, but *History 203* is the name of a specific course.

General:	math
Specific:	Calculus 112
	Advanced Geometry
	Engineering Math

General:	accounting
Specific:	Introductory
	Accounting
	Accounting 321
	Statistics and
	Accounting

General:	geography
Specific:	Climate, Chokepoints,
	and Migrations

General:	biology
Specific:	Biology 102
	Intermediate Biology

You always capitalize the names of courses that are themselves derived from proper nouns; in these examples, the names of languages:

- ☞ I am taking *Spanish 213* this fall.
- ☞ I enjoy studying *Spanish.*
- ☞ My *English 336* class is very difficult.
- ☞ Cecil has an *English* class on Thursday evening.

★

QUESTION: Yesterday, I read a newspaper article that kept mentioning the *East Coast.* I didn't think the directional words *north, south, east,* and *west* were supposed to be capitalized. Am I right?

DR. GRAMMAR: Actually, the newspaper reference was correct, but you are also essentially correct in what you think. General directions are not capitalized.

- ☞ Drive *north* for ten miles and then turn *east.*
- ☞ I live on the *west* side of town.
- ☞ The river runs *southwest* through the small community.

But labels that are associated with specific regions of the country are capitalized.

- ☞ The *Pacific Northwest* provides the consumer with a variety of crabs not found in any other part of the country.
- ☞ The *Eastern Shore* is also famous for delicious seafood, especially crab.

☞ I'm eager to see the pueblos of the *Southwest.*
☞ The people of *Southern California* are gearing up for the next big earthquake.
☞ The *South* has a tradition of warm hospitality.
☞ I live on the *South Side* of Chicago.

★

QUESTION: I remember someone once telling me that *mother* and *father* were capitalized only if the intention was to show extreme respect to them; otherwise, they should not be capitalized. Do you agree?

DR. GRAMMAR: This sounds to Dr. Grammar like one of those nice little rules that too many of us were taught when we were young. While it may be a valid part of someone's etiquette, it certainly does not come from any formal application of English usage.

The way you write father or mother is really quite simple. If it is used in place of a proper name, capitalize it; otherwise, do not. Think of the first names of your mother and father; now see how easily you can substitute them in these sentences:

☞ I hope that *Mother* bakes her famous apple pie for Thanksgiving. [I hope that *Agnes (Elizabeth, Dorothy, etc.)* bakes her famous apple pie for Thanksgiving.]
☞ I must ask *Father* for his advice before I buy my first car. [I must ask *David (Frank, Paul, Roger, etc.)* for his advice before I buy my first car.]
☞ Don't forget to remind *Mother* of the luncheon.

mother or Mother?

☞ Tell *Father* I will call him just as soon as I get back to college.

In all of the examples, you could use the given name of your mother or father and the sentences would read smoothly. The word *mother* or *father,* then, replaces the given name and should be capitalized.

Do not capitalize *mother* and *father* when they are preceded by a possessive pronoun.

☞ Don't forget to remind *my mother* of the luncheon.

☞ Tell *my father* I will call him just as soon as I get back to college.

☞ Larry calls *his father* at least once a week.

☞ Linda asked if anyone had heard from *her mother.*

Try substituting your parent's given name for *mother* or *father* in the four sentences above. You can't—these sentences just won't work! When a possessive pronoun comes before *mother* or *father,* the word should not be capitalized.

★

QUESTION: When I write about other family members, do I capitalize relatives like *aunt, cousin,* etc.?

DR. GRAMMAR: References to other members of your family are capitalized only when they come immediately before the person's name; they then technically become a part of the name.

☞ I hope *Aunt Helena* doesn't try to repair the toaster herself.

aunt or Aunt?

☞ I am expecting *Cousin Eugene, Grandfather Harry,* and *Uncle Billy* to watch the ball game with me on Sunday.

Do not capitalize the family reference if a proper name does not go along with it.

☞ I hope *my aunt* doesn't try to repair the toaster herself.

☞ I am expecting *my cousin, my grandfather,* and *my uncle* to watch the ball game with me on Sunday.

☞ I received a birthday card from *an uncle* whom I had not heard from in fifteen years.

★

QUESTION: What is the present thinking about forming the possessive of a word ending with *s?* I still remember the debate from my high-school days. Is it John *Keats'* poem or *Keats's?*

DR. GRAMMAR: Although there is still some disagreement about this, the guidelines are relatively simple for a regular singular noun. If you form a new syllable in pronouncing the possessive, add *'s.*

☞ my *boss's* travel schedule
☞ *Dallas's* skyline
☞ *Paris's* restaurants
☞ the *witness's* testimony

If you do not pronounce an additional syllable with the possessive, or if the extra syllable would make the word sound strange, it is deleted and a simple apostrophe follows the final *s* in the word.

☞ *Los Angeles'* smog
☞ *Mrs. Hastings'* committee
☞ *Jesus'* parables
☞ *New Orleans'* jazz

The concern, then, comes down to pronunciation. Do you say *Keats's* with two syllables or *Keats'* with one? Dr. Grammar hopes you like *Keats'* poetry as much as he does and that you remember that even in its possessive form Keats has only one syllable.

★

QUESTION: What is the rule for forming the possessive of a plural noun that ends with *s?*

DR. GRAMMAR: This question is easier than the one above. If a plural noun already ends in *s,* you simply add an apostrophe to form the plural.

☞ the *witnesses'* testimony
☞ the *physicians'* statements
☞ the *counties'* changing needs

★

QUESTION: If a noun is plural but does not end with *s,* how do I write the possessive?

DR. GRAMMAR: These are *irregular nouns,* and the possessive is formed simply by adding *'s* to the plural form.

children*'s*   mice*'s*   geese*'s*

Dr. Grammar would hasten to point out that the guidelines covered under the last two questions will be less confusing if you remember a basic principle: Always form the plural of the noun first, then apply the rule for forming the possessive.

Singular	*Plural*	*Possessive*
child	children	children*'s*
boss	bosses	bosses*'*
witness	witnesses	witnesses*'*
goose	geese	geese*'s*

★

QUESTION: My sister always talks about her mother's-in-law house, her mother's-in-law car, and her mother's-in-law dinner party. She said she learned in high school to make possessive the word that did the possessing, *mother* in this case. I don't think she's right, and we are having a family argument about it.

DR. GRAMMAR: Dr. Grammar prays that you and your sister do not precipitate a major family crisis over this issue, but he will give you a little bit of an edge and tell you that *you* are correct. When you are forming a possessive compound noun, you simply add *'s* to the last element of the compound.

- ☞ mother-in-law*'s* house
- ☞ brother-in-law*'s* car
- ☞ secretary-treasurer*'s* expenses
- ☞ attorney general*'s* task force
- ☞ editor in chief*'s* red pencil

Note, however, that the plural of most compound nouns is formed by adding *s* either to the first or to the more important element.

☞ mothers-in-law
☞ brothers-in-law
☞ secretary-treasurers
☞ attorneys general
☞ editors in chief

★

QUESTION: My new boss is named Jesse Wilson Jr. If I want to write his name in a sentence showing possession, do I add the *'s* to *Wilson* or to *Jr.?*

DR. GRAMMAR: When you want to make possessive a term that ends with an abbreviation or number, you always add *'s* at the end of the complete name.

☞ Jesse Wilson Jr.*'s* party
☞ Jesse Wilson III*'s* party
☞ Jesse Wilson Co.*'s* new address
☞ Jesse Wilson Inc.*'s* new address

★

QUESTION: When my husband and I invite guests to our weekend home, do we write "You are invited to Shelly's and Marshall's home" or "You are invited to Shelly and Marshall's home"?

DR. GRAMMAR: You are almost getting into legal territory here, because the question you are asking deals with separate versus joint ownership. If the two parties jointly share the ownership, you add an *'s* to only the last name.

   ☞ Shelly and Marshall*'s* home
   ☞ Bill and George*'s* project [It's a project they did together.]

If you wish to indicate separate ownership, you make each of the nouns possessive.

   ☞ Tom*'s* and Sally*'s* homes are being redecorated.
   ☞ Bill*'s* and George*'s* projects are both good, but Bill*'s* is more complete.

★

QUESTION: I distinctly remember Mrs. Isaacson, my twelfth-grade English teacher, telling us not to use possessive forms with such words as *day, hour,* or *job.* She said these inanimate nouns didn't own anything, so we should not use the possessive form. But I see such words in the possessive form all the time. Is this now an acceptable practice?

DR. GRAMMAR: When Dr. Grammar went to school, a Mrs. Isaacson told him the same thing. But life has grown a bit simpler and more relaxed since then. Several commonly used inanimate nouns are now regularly written in their possessive form. Among the most frequently used are these:

   ☞ a hard *day's* work
   ☞ an *hour's* pay
   ☞ the *job's* responsibilities
   ☞ a *dollar's* value

☞ this *morning's* weather
☞ my *car's* transmission

★

QUESTION: Has the form for abbreviation of state names changed, or are there now two possible forms? I learned, for example, that *Calif.* was the abbreviation for California. More often than not, I now see it written only as *CA*. Are they both correct? Has *CA* replaced the older *Calif.?*

DR. GRAMMAR: You are making the rather common mistake of confusing the abbreviation of a state's name with the official United States Postal Service designation for the state. They are not the same. The abbreviation for California is still *Calif.* Only the United States Postal Service recognizes the designation *CA.* In order to streamline its system, the postal service devised a scheme to give each state a two-letter designation. You should use that designation for mail going only through the postal service. In all other instances, you should either spell out the name of the state or use the abbreviation as it is given in any good dictionary.

★

QUESTION: Is it permissible to abbreviate street names when I am writing a letter? I seem to recall that one can abbreviate the name in the address portion of the letter but not in the body of the letter itself.

DR. GRAMMAR: Although the practice you describe is sometimes used, the actual guidelines for business letter format are more restrictive. Indeed, those guidelines cover more than the names of the streets. You should not abbreviate the names of cities or the months of the year in either the return address or the inside address of a business letter.

do not write

3845 Leeway Ave.
N.Y., N.Y. 10018
Nov. 22, 1992

do write

3845 Leeway Avenue
New York, NY 10018
November 22, 1992

do not write

2945 E. Leport Ln.
Ft. Worth, Tex. 76115
Mar. 14, 1992

do write

2945 East Leport
Lane
Fort Worth, TX 76115
March 14, 1992

Notice that while you do not abbreviate the name of the city, you may use the official two-letter post office designation for the state. However, you may not use any other abbreviated form for the state. For instance, you may not write *Tex.* for *TX* or *Texas.*

Also, you should not abbreviate the words *Fort, Point,* or *Mount* when they are a part of the city's name (Fort Worth, Point Comfort, Mount Prospect). You do abbreviate *saint* when it is used in an abbreviated manner (St. Louis, St. Petersburg).

Remember, though, that individual users of our language often establish some of their own guidelines or rules. If your supervisor prefers that you abbreviate some parts of a return address or inside address, you should not make a fuss about it. Being absolutely correct may not be nearly so nice as being employed!

SECTION FOUR:

IN WHICH DR. GRAMMAR

ANSWERS QUESTIONS

ABOUT PUNCTUATION

Exclamation point: a period that's blown its top.

—*Stars & Stripes*

QUESTION: In this sentence—"Would you please call my secretary tomorrow morning"—do I place a period or a question mark after *morning*?

DR. GRAMMAR: That's a good question. Are you really asking a question or are you politely giving a request for action, a command? Sometimes, requests or commands are phrased as questions for the sake of politeness or courtesy. Use a period if you want your correspondent to call your secretary tomorrow morning. Use a question mark if you expect your correspondent to have a problem with your request.

☞ Would you please fill out the form in triplicate.

☞ Would you give me ten minutes of your time before you leave.

☞ Would you please clear all schedule changes with Ms. Betters.

The implication in these three examples is that the writer is in the position of superiority. He or she is expecting only a positive response. However, if you feel that your reader might be offended by the declarative form, you can use a question mark. The question mark maintains the courtesy of your request and gives the reader an option.

☞ Would you please fill out the form in triplicate?
☞ Would you give me ten minutes of your time before you leave?
☞ Will you please clear all schedule changes with Ms. Betters?

If you are not certain whether your statement should be a question or a command, rephrase it so that your intentions are clear.

☞ Please fill out the form in triplicate.
☞ I need to see you for ten minutes before you leave today.
☞ I would appreciate it if you cleared all schedule changes with Ms. Betters.

★

QUESTION: What is an indirect question, and how do I punctuate it?

DR. GRAMMAR: Many people get confused by indirect questions because they sound so very much like direct questions. At least a part of the language of every indirect question is the exact language of a direct question. Read the direct questions below and see how their wording is then used as a part of an indirect question.

☞ Direct: When will the Franklin Report be ready?
☞ Indirect: I do not know when the Franklin Report will be ready.

☞ Direct: Why did the St. Louis deal fall through?
☞ Indirect: Why the St. Louis deal fell through is a mystery to us.

☞ Direct: How are we going to finance the trip?
☞ Indirect: The real problem is how are we going to finance the trip.

The indirect question is incorporated into a sentence that makes a declarative statement. No one would expect a specific response to any of the indirect questions listed above. Because the writer is not asking for a direct response from the reader, a period—not a question mark—is used to mark the end of the sentence.

★

QUESTION: Should I place a comma between the adjectives *self-motivated* and *ambitious* in the sentence: "He is a self-motivated ambitious person"?

DR. GRAMMAR: If two adjectives modify the same noun with equal force, place a comma between them. To test for equal force, try placing the conjunction *and* between the adjectives. If the sentence with *and* makes sense, the two adjectives have equal force. In the example above, you can place *and* between *self-motivated* and *ambitious.* You can write: "He is a self-motivated *and* ambitious person."

☞ Mrs. Graff was a charming, hospitable hostess.
☞ Mrs. Graff was a charming *and* hospitable hostess.

☞ Have you seen the new modular office furniture? [Not: Have you seen the new *and* modular office furniture?]
☞ Betty has not done the monthly fiscal report. [Not: Betty has not done the monthly *and* fiscal report.]

Test, too, for adjectives that form a complete unit with the noun and for those places where the noun without the adjective would make no sense or would lose meaning. This is especially important when you have two or more adjectives preceding a noun.

☞ Arthur is a competent, efficient physical therapist.
☞ Be wary of that crotchety little old man in the corner store.

In the first example, *physical* forms a unit with the noun *therapist.* Both words are needed to label the profession: Arthur is a *physical therapist.* In the second example, you could insert an *and* between *little* and *old* and thus make *little* and *old* equal. If you leave out the *and,* you are giving emphasis to the *old man* who also happens to be crotchety and little.

★

QUESTION: Do I place commas around the name *Charmaine* in the sentence: "My sister Charmaine has just married"?

DR. GRAMMAR: This is a particularly good question. There is much confusion with this type of sentence construction. If you do it right, you will provide your reader with some very important information. Placing commas around *Charmaine* depends both on how many sisters you have and how important it is for the person to whom you are writing to know her name. Let's look at the following example:

☞ My sister, Charmaine, has just married.

Writing "My sister, Charmaine, has just married" indicates that you have just one sister and that her name is Charmaine. Placing commas around Charmaine means that you could remove her name in the sentence without losing any meaning or clarity. Including her name provides a little more information.

If you write "My sister Charmaine has just married"— with no commas around Charmaine—you are saying you have more than one sister and that the reader needs to know the name of the sister who just married.

If you set off the name by commas, you are saying that the meaning of the sentence isn't restricted to the name within those commas. In somewhat technical language, the name within the commas is called a *nonrestrictive modifier*. Look at this example:

☞ My wife, Hester, left this morning for Denver.

Remember that if you set off the name by commas, it is a nonrestrictive modifier. That is, the meaning of the sentence is not changed (or restricted) by the name within the commas. Because we assume that you have only one wife, *Hester* is a nonrestrictive modifier. You are simply including the name as a bit of additional information for your reader.

If you do not set off the name by commas, it is a *restrictive modifier*. That is, it changes (or restricts) the meaning of the sentence. Look at these examples:

☞ My sister Eileen is a real card. [Not all of my sisters are cards, just Eileen.]

☞ His friend Gary called from Milwaukee. [He has many friends, but Gary is the one who called.]

★

QUESTION: Do you remember the lyrics in *Funny Girl* that go, "People who need people are the luckiest people in the world"? Should there be a comma after the first *people* and another, a closing comma, after the second *people*? Should it go, "People, who need people, are . . ."?

DR. GRAMMAR: Again, the decision depends on the nature of the phrase; in this example, *who need people.* You must determine if it is essential to the meaning of the sentence. An essential phrase or clause, sometimes called a restrictive phrase or a restrictive clause, is necessary to the meaning of the sentence and is *not* set off by commas.

When you write the sentence "People who need people are the luckiest people in the world," the clause *who need people* is essential to what you are conveying and therefore is *not* enclosed in commas. Remove the clause from the sentence and you can see that the meaning is lost: "People are the luckiest people in the world." But you don't mean to say that. You don't mean to say that all people are the luckiest people in the world. You mean to say that just those people who need other people are the luckiest people in the world.

Look at this example:

☞ Employees who are habitually late will be fired.

Not all employees will be fired, only those who are habitually late. That bit of information, so important to the meaning of the sentence, is contained in the essential or restrictive clause *who are habitually late.*

☞ Money that is not well spent is lost money.

Here, again, the meaning of the sentence is restricted to the essential phrase *that is well spent.* You certainly would not want the sentence to read simply "Money is lost money."

★

QUESTION: I had a teacher in high school who made quite an issue about the distinction between *that* and *which.* What is the distinction and is it still valid? (I can't remember it at all; I just remember Mrs. Lorenz spending hours reviewing it with us.)

DR. GRAMMAR: Bless Mrs. Lorenz. She was probably doing a good job of differentiating between the two words, and, believe me, there used to be a very distinct and formal guideline. Like so much else about our language, guidelines change and relax with time. About all you need to remember about *that* and *which* is to use *that* for restrictive (essential) clauses and *which* for nonrestrictive (nonessential) ones. It is a distinction still practiced by careful writers and speakers.

☞ The book *that* I borrowed from Leslie was stolen.

You are telling your reader that the book you borrowed from Leslie was the book that was stolen, not the one you borrowed from anyone else.

☞ The book, *which* I borrowed from Leslie, was stolen.

Now you are telling your reader that the book was stolen and that it just happened to be the one you borrowed from Leslie. You really want to tell the reader about the stolen book; the fact that the book belonged to Leslie is of secondary importance.

As you can see, you have the grammatical means to make your message absolutely clear. By using *that* or *which,* you can inform the reader whether the information in the clause is or is not essential for proper understanding.

☞ The company's legal department, *which* is on the twelfth floor, was damaged by fire over the weekend.

If you take out the *which* clause—this is suggested as a possibility by the use of commas—the sentence declares that the company has one legal department and it was damaged by fire.

☞ The company's legal department *that* is on the twelfth floor was damaged by fire over the weekend.

With the use of *that,* and without the use of commas, your reader will see that the company's legal department had offices on other floors, too, but only the ones on the twelfth floor were damaged.

☞ The legal department *that* Mr. Fawcett heads does not handle letters from our readers.

Mr. Fawcett's legal department does not handle letters from readers, but the sentence does not say that *none* of the legal departments handles such correspondence; only Mr. Fawcett's department doesn't deal with it.

☞ The legal department, *which* Ms. Ramirez heads, does not handle letters from readers.

Take out the clause *which Ms. Ramirez heads* and the sentence reads, "The legal department does not handle letters from readers." This means the entire legal department does not handle such mail.

Correctly using *that* and *which* is just one more way you can help your reader to get the meaning you intend to communicate.

★

QUESTION: Have I placed commas correctly in the sentence "August 3, 1898, was an important date in the history of the Jones Ballbearing Company"?

COMMAS IN DATES

133

DR. GRAMMAR: Yes, you have. Traditionally, the year has been considered to be in apposition (equal in position) to the month and the day. Appositional words and phrases are set off by commas.

☞ I was born on January 14, 1944, in Kansas City, Missouri.

☞ On July 20, 1994, we shall celebrate the twenty-fifth anniversary of the first moonwalk.

However, if you write only the month and the year and do not include a specific date, you do not use a comma:

☞ That topic was covered in the March 1988 issue of *Music* magazine.

☞ I still remember the day in August 1978 when I began my job at Sears.

★

QUESTION: How should we write the name of our new company? Do we put a comma before the *and*? Should we write "Jones, Thomas, and Halsey" or "Jones, Thomas and Halsey"?

DR. GRAMMAR: That's up to the founders of the company. Should they decide to have a comma in the name, that'll be the style, and everyone who writes to the company for the next jillion years must use it. Writing the three names with or without the second comma is a matter of choice, and either option would be considered correct. You can set the pattern for the company, at least until someone else makes another decision about the company's name. Certainly, if you work for a company that already has the comma in place, you must use it. If the company does not have a comma in its title, you should not take it upon yourself to insert one.

Actually, you bring up the old problem of the use of commas in a series. Is it a "bacon, lettuce, and tomato sandwich" or is it a "bacon, lettuce and tomato sandwich"?

For the most part, writers and editors are flexible about the use of serial commas. Traditionalists *never* omit the comma, but other writers do. My own preference, again for *clarity,* is to use serial commas.

☞ Do not fold, spindle, or mutilate.
☞ On the trip to Kokomo, you will need to bring along your breakfast, lunch, and dinner.
☞ The reception will be hosted by the Galens, the Budds, and the Fiores.

Whatever your preference for serial commas, you must use them when they are needed to avoid confusion. Look at this example:

☞ Mary, LaVerne and Kim called me yesterday.

As written, this sentence has two possible meanings. The writer may be addressing Mary and telling her that LaVerne and Kim called yesterday. Or the writer may be saying that three people—Mary, LaVerne, and Kim—called yesterday. If the writer intends this latter meaning, a comma before the *and* makes it the only possible meaning and, thus, the one to use: Mary, LaVerne, and Kim.

★

QUESTION: I work in an accounting office where my immediate supervisor retains the abbreviation for *Junior* in his name. How do I punctuate it when I write a memo to him?

DR. GRAMMAR: The general guideline is that you should not use a comma. *Junior, Senior,* or even roman numerals after an individual's name are considered a part of that person's name.

- ☞ Jason Samuel Sr.
- ☞ Francis McDonald Jr.
- ☞ Vincent Brannigan III
- ☞ Caspar Singleton 2d

However, if your supervisor wants a comma before the appendage, use one. If Mr. Samuel wishes you to use a comma when you type his name, you should accept his wishes and type *Jason Samuel, Sr.* If a title follows the name, punctuate it like this: *Jason Samuel, Sr., Director of Marketing.* You do not use the second comma if you also need to use a possessive ending: *Jason Samuel, Sr.'s report is at the print shop right now.*

★

QUESTION: Should I use commas when I abbreviate titles?

DR. GRAMMAR: Set off by commas abbreviations of titles, academic degrees, and religious orders.

- ☞ Peter Hoskins, Esq., will address our annual meeting next month. [*Esq.,* of course, is the abbreviation for *Esquire.*]
- ☞ Sr. Agnes, O.S.B., will give a presentation to the

committee at the end of the month. [*Sr.* is the abbreviation for *Sister,* a Catholic nun, and *O.S.B.* is the abbreviation for the *Order of St. Benedict,* the religious order to which Sr. Agnes belongs.]

☞ Donald W. Wall, M.D., will speak at the newly formed substance-abuse clinic next Thursday.

★

QUESTION: I know that if I address a person by name at the beginning of a sentence, I should follow that name with a comma: "Scott, here's the magazine." But do I separate the name from the rest of the sentence if it is at the end? For example, "Here's the magazine, Scott."

DR. GRAMMAR: Yes, indeed. When you call someone by his or her name in a sentence, you use what is called a *noun of address.* The noun of address is set off from the rest of the sentence by commas no matter where it occurs, even if it appears in the middle of the sentence.

☞ *Brian,* can you come here and give me a hand?

☞ Can you come here and give me a hand, *Brian?*

☞ Can you come here, *Brian,* and give me a hand?

★

QUESTION: Someone told me that a prepositional phrase at the beginning of a sentence should be followed by a comma. Is that correct?

DR. GRAMMAR: You usually do not separate short prepositional phrases that occur at the beginning of a sentence from the rest of the sentence. For example:

☞ *Before the test* I thought I knew all of the answers.
☞ *In the corner* he planted a large rose bush.

If the introductory prepositional phrase is a long one, you should follow it with a comma. It'll give the reader a chance to catch his or her breath.

☞ *Before the test on the American short story last Wednesday,* I thought I knew all of the answers.
☞ *In the sunny and much-pampered corner of the yard,* he planted a large rose bush.

★

QUESTION: I can never seem to figure out when or how to punctuate such words as *however, therefore,* and *of course* when I use them internally in a sentence. Are they ever set off by commas?

DR. GRAMMAR: You are addressing two categories of words here. The first group is called transitional markers and includes such words as *however, nevertheless, therefore,* and *on the other hand.* The second group is recognized as independent comments and includes such words as *of course, in my opinion,* and *obviously.* They clearly express your personal interpretation or evaluation. For both categories of words, you use commas to set off the material when it is nonessential to the meaning of the sentence and seems to disrupt the flow of the sentence. Do not use commas when the material is important to the meaning of the sentence. If you read the following sentence sets aloud, you will see that your voice rises ever so slightly when you are reading the essential words or phrases and drops ever so slightly when you are reading the nonessential ones.

☞ Essential: I am nevertheless fully committed to the second half of your plan.

☞ Nonessential: I believe, nevertheless, that the program will be cost effective.

☞ Essential: It is of course vitally important that you keep me closely informed about the progress of the effort.

☞ Nonessential: I think that you, of course, would want to send daily updates to all department managers.

★

QUESTION: I copied two sentences from our company's newsletter so I could ask you about them. Why do commas appear in each of them? I can't see any reason for their use.

☞ Ms. Leib said she wanted her staff members to enjoy the training sessions, not to dread them.

☞ Employees should use the FAX equipment, not the modem, to transmit information to the Boston office.

DR. GRAMMAR: Commas were needed in the two sentences to mark elements of contrast. When commas are so used, they change the way the sentence is to be read, as they give emphasis to the contrasting elements. Here are some more examples:

☞ I asked you to bring white, not red, wine to the party.

☞ It was Dr. Waldstein, not Dr. Roberts, who prescribed the exercise therapy.

The contrasting factor can change the sentence from a simple, declarative statement to a question. Examine these examples:

☞ I hope we can leave work early next Friday, don't you?

☞ This is a good place for a quick lunch, isn't it?

★

QUESTION: I thought that a comma was always used to separate the parts of a compound sentence joined by *and*. My son showed me his English paper, and the sentence "William Faulkner wrote many short stories and novels about the Old South, and easily became its primary literary voice in the twentieth century" was marked incorrect because of the comma. I don't understand why.

DR. GRAMMAR: The problem is a rather common one, and you are correct: A comma is used to separate the two parts of a compound sentence joined by *and*. But your son did not write a compound sentence. He simply used two verbs—*wrote* and *became*—with his subject, *Faulkner*. A compound sentence must contain two or more independent clauses, each having a subject and a verb. Your son's sentence has only one subject and two verbs. Study the differences in the following sentence pairs:

☞ William Faulkner wrote many short stories and novels about the Old South and easily became its primary literary voice in the twentieth century.

☞ William Faulkner wrote many short stories and novels about the Old South, and *he* easily became its primary literary voice in the twentieth century.

☞ The quarterly report must be typed onto the designated forms and should be mailed to all offices by the fifth day of each month.

☞ The quarterly report must be typed onto the designated forms, and *it* should be mailed to all offices by the fifth day of each month.

★

QUESTION: Yesterday, I wrote the following sentence in a report: "Ask the maintenance department to increase trash pickups and ask the security director to reinstate its floor-monitoring system." One of the aides here insisted that I should have a comma after *pickups* and before *and.* I don't think so. What do you think?

DR. GRAMMAR: Dr. Grammar must take the side of the aide in this dispute. When you have a sentence in which at least one verb is in the imperative (giving a command) and no subject is expressed, you should treat the sentence as if it were a compound sentence and separate the clauses with a comma.

☞ Ask the maintenance department to increase trash pickups, and ask the security director to reinstate its floor-monitoring system.

☞ Examine the materials I am sending you, and call me to schedule an appointment so we can discuss them.

☞ You should finish the sketches by Thursday afternoon, but please call me if you are going to be delayed.

★

QUESTION: Don't I always need to use commas to set off the word *too* from the rest of the sentence?

DR. GRAMMAR: Let me see if I can separate the situations for you. When *too* is used to mean "also," it is usually set off from the rest of the sentence by commas.

☞ I, too, want you to be recognized for your work.
☞ The fact remains that you, too, could be successful with hard work.

However, when *too* comes at the end of a clause or a sentence, the comma is typically omitted.

☞ We have a new puppy at our house too.
☞ His office staff works hard too, but they never seem to accomplish as much as they should.

Of course, you must remember that when *too* is used to mean "excessively," no commas are used.

☞ It was just too hot in the room for me to work.
☞ The bearings were too worn to be functional.

★

QUESTION: My old grammar handbook says that a comma should be employed to avoid a misreading. But I never know when something is going to be misread, so I never know when to use a comma. Can that rule be made more specific?

DR. GRAMMAR: If you remember to think of punctuation marks as road signs, I think you will more clearly see how to use the rule. Sometimes it is necessary to let your reader know when to slow down in order to get the correct meaning. Read the following sentence without thinking too much about it:

> **x** I guess for someone religious like Father Brian Lewis is just another challenge.

Dr. Grammar suspects that you read "Father Brian Lewis" all in one sweep and considered it the name of the priest, and that you also wondered if a word was missing from the sentence. Look at how the simple comma changes the meaning of the sentence:

> ☞ I guess for someone religious like Father Brian, Lewis is just another challenge.

Now the sentence says something quite different. The priest's name is Father Brian; Lewis is another person.

Here are a couple of other examples to demonstrate how one can misread a sentence if it doesn't have the appropriate road sign in place—in these cases, a comma:

> **x** I argue that all any car is is a nuisance.
> ☞ I argue that all any car is, is a nuisance.

✗ Soon after the report was published by someone in the personnel department.

☞ Soon after, the report was published by someone in the personnel department.

★

QUESTION: Isn't there a rule that says the subject of a sentence and the verb must not be separated by a comma?

DR. GRAMMAR: You are partially correct. The rule actually says that you should not separate the subject of a sentence from its verb by a *single* comma. If you remember that guideline, you will avoid the punctuation errors that appear in the following two sentences:

✗ My cousin from Milwaukee, called to invite me up for a weekend.

✗ The pecan pie recipe, belonged to my grand-mother.

There are, of course, times when you use a pair of commas to separate material that comes between the subject and the verb.

☞ My cousin, who is from Milwaukee, called to invite me up for a weekend.

☞ The pecan pie recipe, which you found in the kitchen cabinet, belonged to my grandmother.

The rule you asked about has two other parts. One says that you should never use a comma to separate a verb from its object. These sentences are punctuated *incorrectly:*

x Our team easily won, the game.

x My teacher thinks, that everyone should be able to pass the exam next week.

And the third part of the rule suggests that you should never use a comma to separate a verb from its complement. *Never* punctuate a sentence as follows:

x The flowers in her yard are, absolutely beautiful.

x The banquet table looked, inviting with all of its luscious food and its beautiful ice carvings.

★

QUESTION: Do I use a comma before the *Inc.* when it is part of a company's official name?

DR. GRAMMAR: The *general* rule is not to use a comma in this instance. But, once again, you should use the format that is preferred by the individual company. The publishing giant Time preferred no comma. Its corporate title was written like this:

☞ Time Inc.

The publishing company Prentice-Hall, on the other hand, uses the comma in its official title. Its official company title is written like this:

☞ Prentice-Hall, Inc.

★

QUESTION: I've never understood the semicolon and when to use it.

DR. GRAMMAR: I'll try to help. The four major marks of punctuation—the comma, the semicolon, the colon, and the period—are used in writing as traffic signs are used on a road. They inform a reader what is going to happen next; maybe there is going to be a change of direction in the way the sentence is moving, or perhaps a list of specifics is going to follow.

Years ago, these marks of punctuation were taught like the rest stops of music. Students were taught to pause and to count "one" silently when they read a comma, to count to two for a semicolon, to three for a colon, and to four for a period. We do not use this system any longer, but it is a good one to help us to know the relative strength and weakness of the marks. Remember that the comma is the weakest of all possible marks of punctuation and that the period is the strongest.

The most common use of the semicolon is to join two short, related, and grammatically equal sentences to make a longer one.

☞ We worked all day on the proposal. It is finally ready for Mr. Jackob's approval.

☞ We worked all day on the proposal; it is finally ready for Mr. Jackob's approval.

The ideas in the two sentences are related, so you should join them into a single sentence with a semicolon.

☞ Mary attended the meeting in Atlanta; Steve was delayed by the storm in Chicago.

☞ I requested three new assistants for the front office; all were approved.

Sometimes, you can help your reader see the relationship between the two sentences you are joining by using a conjunction that expresses that relationship. In those instances, you typically have a semicolon in front of the conjunction and a comma after it.

☞ We worked all day on the proposal; therefore, it is finally ready for Mr. Jackob's approval.

☞ Mary got to the meeting in Atlanta; however, Steve was delayed by the storm in Chicago.

The semicolon can also function as a kind of *supercomma*. Remember what I said about the relative strength of the marks of punctuation: If you have commas at other points in the sentence, you may need to use a semicolon at places where you need a stronger mark. Use the semicolon to separate items in a series if those items already contain commas.

☞ This year, we have opened branch stores in Lincoln, Nebraska; Topeka, Kansas; Pueblo, Colorado; and Laramie, Wyoming.

☞ Peabrook and Company was represented by Martha Smith, Director of Special Affairs; Helene Bonds, Coordinator of Sales Research; and George Brookfield, Coordinator for Community Outreach.

And the semicolon is used when two separate sentences are joined by expressions such as *for example, that is,* or *namely.*

☞ Harry is a conscientious worker; for example, he routinely stays past seven o'clock to get a head start on his next day's assignment.

☞ You must learn to live with your decision; namely, *you* hired Peter.

☞ Please fill out the complete application; that is, do not leave any questions unanswered.

As always, there can be exceptions, especially when the clauses are unusually short and there is no possibility of confusion.

☞ Cory would like to go to Yale, Jack is talking about Brown, and Gwen has already decided on Colgate.

☞ We cleaned up the mess quickly because Kathy washed the dishes, Jack dried them, and I put them away.

★

QUESTION: Is a colon used only to introduce lists? Can it be used to join separate sentences?

DR. GRAMMAR: The colon is basically used to introduce a series or a statement at the end of a complete clause.

☞ I have three favorite writers: Yeats, the poet; James, the novelist; and Chekhov, the playwright.

☞ The Board of Directors will meet on the following dates: Monday, January 20; Wednesday, May 25; and Wednesday, September 24.

Do not use a colon if the series follows a verb or a preposition.

☞ The committee consisted of Ms. Buller, Mr. Jenkins, Dr. Connors, and Rev. Hopwell.

☞ The collection includes three lithographs, six oils, and one pen-and-ink drawing.

However, use a colon after a verb when the items in a series are presented in list form.

☞ The collection included:
  18 lithographs
  38 oils
  21 acrylics
  7 pen-and-ink drawings.

It is also used to introduce a quotation:

☞ She startled the audience with her statement: "I hate you all for what I have heard you say here this evening!"

And it can be used to give emphasis to an amplification:

☞ I have in mind only one goal: I want to be president of this company within five years.

★

QUESTION: In high school I learned to put a colon in the salutation of a business letter, but I see many letters without the colon. Is this a trend?

DR. GRAMMAR: The traditional and most common format for business letters requires a colon after the salutation.

☞ Dear Dr. Presley:
☞ Dear Ms. McDonald:

However, like everything else, styles change, and you must make decisions. One format currently popular for business-letter writing is the full-block format. Everything in the letter is blocked against the left margin and no paragraphs are indented. Quite often in this format, the colon is not used after the salutation.

☞ Dear Dr. Presley
☞ Dear Ms. McDonald

★

QUESTION: When I am writing a report on a book I have read, how do I show the difference between the title and the subtitle?

DR. GRAMMAR: You always differentiate the title from the subtitle by placing a colon between them.

☞ *The Why of Where: Geography for the Billions*
☞ *Structures: A Guide for the Small Business Office*
☞ *Wallace Stevens: The Man and the Poet*
☞ *Contact: A Textbook in Applied Communication*

★

QUESTION: My boss told me that I should capitalize any word that comes immediately after a colon. I think this is incorrect. What do you think?

DR. GRAMMAR: Whether you capitalize the first word following a colon depends on the text.

You should not capitalize the first word after a colon if it does not begin a complete sentence.

☞ I need two courses to complete my degree: mathematics and geography.

You must, of course, capitalize words if they are proper nouns.

☞ I need two courses to complete my degree: Mathematics 241 and French 314.

You should not capitalize the first word of an independent clause after a colon if the clause is used to explain an aspect of the first part.

☞ Margo and Harry have conflicting points of view: she prefers to have parties catered, but he wants to do them by himself.

You *do* capitalize the first word of an independent clause following a colon if what follows is a rule or a principle.

☞ Follow this rule: Check all bags as you enter the store.

☞ I have just one point to make: No one is to sign a payroll voucher without my approval.

You should also capitalize the first word of an independent clause that follows a colon when the material after the colon is two or more sentences.

☞ Follow these rules: Check all bags as you enter the store. Keep your claim check with you at all times.

☞ Here's our new procedure: First, review all application files. Second, select at least six qualified applicants. Third, have Lynn schedule interviews. Fourth, notify Mr. McKeever of the times and dates.

Capitalize, too, when the first word after the colon introduces a quotation.

☞ Carl's message was certainly clear enough: "If you choose Ed to work on the Orlando project, I quit!"

★

QUESTION: At times I see brackets around a word or a phrase and at other times parentheses. Does it really matter which I use?

DR. GRAMMAR: Actually, *brackets* and *parentheses* have quite different functions in a sentence. You should use parentheses to set off explanatory or qualifying information from the rest of the sentence.

☞ By Tuesday evening (or at the very latest Wednesday morning) I need your report on my desk.
☞ By Wednesday morning (and I don't mean afternoon) I must have your report on my desk.

If the parenthetical material is a complete sentence, you do not use a period, but you can use a question mark or an exclamation point if one should be appropriate.

☞ By Wednesday morning (if you value your job!) I must have your report on my desk.
☞ I finally found the job description (was it the one that Jayne wrote?) on top of my file cabinet.

Brackets, too, are used to insert information that may be useful into a sentence. Brackets enclose information, corrections, queries, and so forth, provided by someone other than the writer of the text (or the speaker, if the material is a quote). Someone other than the author of the following sentence might insert [Texas] to avoid possible confusion with Paris, France.

☞ My aunt is proud that she has lived for seventy-five years in Paris [Texas] and has never been to a big city.

Someone other than the source of each of the quotes below would insert the bracketed material for clarity.

☞ My aunt is proud that she has "... lived for seventy-five years in Paris [Texas] and [has] never been to a big city."
☞ President Bush said, "He [Vice President Quayle] has authorization to represent me in this matter."

Place brackets around the Latin word *sic,* meaning "thus," when you quote something that contains an error. You do this to show your reader that you know there is an error but that you are obligated to write it exactly as it is in the original because you are quoting directly.

☞ "The principle [*sic*] will be out of the school until July 21."
☞ The brochure announced, "We will reach our happy destination in Miama [*sic*] just before sundown."

★

QUESTION: Sometimes I feel a need to emphasize something I am saying in a sentence. Can I use parentheses or dashes to do it? What about underlining it?

DR. GRAMMAR: Probably the easiest way to emphasize material is to use dashes. Because parentheses are used with qualifying or explanatory material, they actually weaken something instead of intensifying it. Dashes intensify it.

☞ By Tuesday—and I really mean Tuesday—I must have your report.

☞ If the weather is unusually hot—and I'll be the judge of that—jackets will not be required in the office.

If you want to emphasize something, you must select carefully and use emphasis sparingly. If you emphasize everything, or too much, you'll lose the effect of your emphasis—if you know what I mean.

★

QUESTION: If a sentence ends with a quotation, does the period go inside or outside the closing quotation marks?

DR. GRAMMAR: In American usage the period always goes inside the closing quotation marks.

☞ The poet wrote, "Give me the balm of an easy sleep."

☞ Our supervisor said, "I insist that everyone keep a

careful written record of all telephone conversa-
tions for the next week."

☞ "I will go with you," she said, "if you think I can
make a contribution at the meeting."

★

QUESTION: Isn't there some special rule about how we are
supposed to use question marks and exclamation points
when they are used in direct quotations? I remember being
terribly confused in high school by all of this.

DR. GRAMMAR: You were confused because the issue is
confusing. Where you place either of these marks of punctuation—the question mark or the exclamation point—depends on what part of the sentence is a question or what part
is an exclamation.

Let's deal with the question mark first. If only the quoted
matter is a question, the question mark goes inside the quotation marks to show that it clearly belongs to the quotation.

☞ Harry asked, "Did you mail the package to Omaha
yesterday or the day before?"

☞ Martha replied, "Yesterday. Do you need a copy of
the shipping invoice?"

Because the quoted material in each example is a question,
the closing quotation marks go outside the question mark.

If the entire statement, and not just the quoted material,
is a question, the question mark goes outside the closing
quotation marks to show that it belongs to the entire sentence.

☞ Did you hear Howard last week when he said, "I will quit within three months if they don't give me a raise"?

☞ Who was it who said, "Have it your way"?

The exclamation point follows the same rules with quotation marks as does the question mark. If the quotation itself is exclamatory, place the exclamation point inside the quotation marks.

☞ "I quit!" she exclaimed.

☞ "Call the police!" he screamed.

If the entire statement is exclamatory, place the exclamation point outside the quotation marks.

☞ My name is Thomas; never call me "Tom"!

☞ Good grief. She actually said, "I love you"!

By the way, be careful with the use of the exclamation point. If you use it too often, you weaken its effectiveness.

★

QUESTION: My literature teacher circled some colons and semicolons that I had used incorrectly with quotation marks in my last paper. Is there some special way these are to be used?

DR. GRAMMAR: Yes, there are guidelines for how you should use the colon and the semicolon with quotation marks, and they are quite simple. Unlike the period and the comma, the colon and the semicolon *always* go outside the quotation marks.

☞ Mr. Simmons gave us three concepts "to ponder carefully": (a) thesis, (b) antithesis, and (c) synthesis.

☞ George warned us about the "three-hour and three-martini lunch"; ignoring him, we put our jobs at risk.

☞ The advertisement said, "Reach out and touch someone"; we did—now look at our phone bill!

★

QUESTION: If I use a direct quotation in a piece of my own writing and want to leave a part of it out, what do I put into the sentence to indicate that I am skipping material? Is that where *sic* comes in?

DR. GRAMMAR: Yes, there is something you should use to indicate you have omitted material from a direct quotation, but no, it is not *sic*. (For the correct use of *sic*, see page 153.) What you use is a set of *ellipsis points*. The set of ellipsis points consists of three periods with spaces before, between, and after them. This punctuation will indicate clearly to your reader exactly where you have omitted material.

☞ The article about America's involvement in the drug war quotes Senator Neilson as saying, "The most important thing we have to keep in our minds today . . . is that we are at war and it is a war we must win."

If the omitted material is at the end of a sentence, use the three ellipsis points and add whatever appropriate mark of punctuation (a period, a question mark, or an exclamation point) is needed to end the sentence.

ELLIPSIS POINTS

☞ Coach Daggert said, "If this team hasn't any more pride than I've seen tonight, we can forget winning the division and we can even forget winning the next game. I've never seen such a lack of dedication. . . ."

★

QUESTION: I'm writing a paper for my sociology class and want to use a sentence that is a question; it contains a quotation that is a direct question. Do I use two question marks to show that two questions are involved?

DR. GRAMMAR: No. Keep life simple. You should never use double question marks. Do *not* write something like this:

✗ Was she the one who asked, "Where have all the dictionaries gone?"?

Instead, use only one question mark, like this:

☞ Was she the one who asked, "Where have all the dictionaries gone"?

Notice that the question mark is placed outside the closing quotation marks to show that it goes with the *whole* sentence.

POSTSCRIPT

Well, if you have read this far, you must be "grammared out." (Did he use *grammar* as a verb? Can he *do* that?) This is just a sampling of the questions I receive on The Write Line at Oakton Community College. My responses are based on my knowledgeable perceptions of the workings of the English language. I am not the only authority; I am not the final authority. Many so-called experts disagree; many of you, I am sure, may disagree with some of my answers. Out of such disagreement dialog is born, change occurs.

As I look back over these pages, I have the sense that I have sometimes given rather harsh prescriptions for what are surely subjective ailments. After all, is there an absolutely "right" way to say something? Haven't poets, philosophers, politicians, even movie stars altered our sense of the language so radically over the last hundred years that one cannot ever place oneself in such a position of hubris as mine in this guidebook?

Well, yes and no. I've been a serious observer of the English language for over two decades, and my goal as a student and as a teacher has always been simply to make everything perfectly clear. Grammar and usage are nothing so much as the attempt to create order and clarity out of the chaos of thoughts and ideas, so that everyone knows exactly what is being said.

And though there are aspects of this debate that verge on mere opinion, there are some points that are definitively "right" or "wrong." *Usage* is the ultimate barometer of right or wrong; what is wrong today might be right tomorrow if the "wrong" form is used often enough. After all, in the Middle Ages a person described as "nice" was branded as being foolish or stupid. Are we really going to keep insisting that *impact* cannot be used as a verb, when everyone from your plumber to the President insists on using it as such? What about all the foreign words that have crept into the English language as a result of immigration, words like *schlepp, yenta,* and *klutz* from Yiddish; *macho* from Spanish; and, most recently, *perestroika* and *glasnost* from Russian? And there's my own personal "usage barometer." I was once asked by an editor to "hip up" my somewhat formal prose. I must say that I did not know that my anatomy had anything to do with my writing style—if I may get that affront off my chest.

For the sake of sanity, and of our common culture, we have to agree on what linguists call "language etiquette." Often, this involves keeping a mind open to change. Modifications in language happen ever so slowly; a glance in any English dictionary demonstrates the sluggish rate of change.

Purists will always—and *should* always—fight the good fight, but one cannot ignore advertisements, movie and book titles, and televisionspeak. It is the transition period that is so awkward, the interlude in which usage moves from what was totally "wrong" to what is acceptable and eventually "correct."

The most important fact I hope my readers take from this guide is that basic mastery of the complexity of the English language yields an ability to bend the rules a bit. Robert Frost once said that writing poetry without meter is like playing tennis without a net. I feel one must know the dimensions of the net before one can take it down. In getting the "writes" from the "wrongs," there are ample rewards.

I should like to invite you to send me your questions about the English language. If I did not cover some of your concerns or pet peeves in this edition, perhaps I can get to them in a future book.

"Dr. Grammar"
c/o Vintage Books, Random House, Inc.
201 East 50th Street, 28th floor
New York, New York 10022

ABOUT THE AUTHOR

★

RICHARD FRANCIS TRACZ is professor of English and chairman of the department at Oakton Community College in Illinois, where he also serves as Dr. Grammar on The Write Line, a telephone question-and-answer service provided by the college. He is the author of nine college-level writing texts and is a frequent speaker at professional writing conferences and workshops. A teacher of writing for a quarter century, he draws upon his vast classroom experience, his scholarship, and his ready wit to answer the dozens of questions put to Dr. Grammar each day.

ABOUT THE PRODUCER

★

JEROME AGEL has written and produced more than forty major books, including collaborations with Marshall McLuhan, Carl Sagan, Herman Kahn, Stanley Kubrick, R. Buckminster Fuller, and Isaac Asimov. His two nonfiction novels were the highly praised *22 Fires* and *Deliverance in Shanghai* (cowritten with Eugene Boe). His new works include *Where on Earth?*, *Cleopatra's Nose . . .*, *Why in the World* (with George Demko), *Our Fifty States*, *12 Documents That Changed the World*, *100 Amazing Americans*, and *Amending America: How the American People Have Reshaped the Constitution to Their Changing Needs* (with Richard B. Bernstein). *The U.S. Constitution for Everyone* is in its fifteenth printing. Books to be published include *The Native American Encyclopedia*.